BORN A GIRL

It Takes Courage

By Alice Dussutour

TRANSLATED FROM FRENCH
by David Warriner

ORCA BOOK PUBLISHERS

FOREWORD

"It's a girl!" Chances are when many biologically female babies are born, these three simple words will be said by a parent, midwife or someone else helping with the birth.

Okay, so it's a girl. Now what? There's a whole life story waiting to be written for these girls, filled with hopes, dreams, doubts, fears and love.

And depending on where in the world these girls are born, their experience of being a girl will be different. Their lives will be shaped by different expectations and taboos and influenced by not only their own desires but also those of their parents and others around them.

Alice Dussutour explores the challenges and the beauty of being born a girl. She introduces us to five girls from around the world who share what it means for them to grow up in the countries they live in—countries where being a girl often still means they are forced to live a lesser life.

She exposes what's hard for them, the forbidden things, the burdens of tradition, the humiliation. How many girls will be horrified to see their body bleeding one day, like Kaneila? How many will use their keys as a weapon to defend themselves when walking the streets, like Luisa? How many will find themselves preoccupied by their weight, like Jade?

These are concerns for girls who are alive today. And we should also remember that there are some girls who will never enter this world because they are unwanted in pregnancy.

Still, Dussutour finds a way to show us the lighter, freer sides of being a girl too. There are women who help, who protect and who lead by example. "The manager of the sanctuary is a woman," says Makena, seeing a future for herself in caring for animals. Some streets are dangerous, Luisa finds, but there are also places where girls can stand up and fight for their rights. And where there are restrictions, there is also freedom, we learn from Mahnoosh, who enjoys a double life as a boy.

One girl's story at a time, Dussutour shows us the individual and collective realities of what it means to be born a girl. The pages in her book carry facts and fiction, words and pictures, to give us a glimpse into the world of five girls who have one thing in common despite living very different lives.

There is a message about sorority (sisterhood) in this book, and it's a complex one. The author isn't saying, "We're all the same, so let's work together." She's saying, "I know we're not the same, but I'm trying to understand your experience in life. As a sister, I feel for you. I know your anger, and I share your dreams."

Happy reading, sisters and allies!

—*Clementine Beauvais*, children's author and lecturer at the University of York, England

CONTENTS

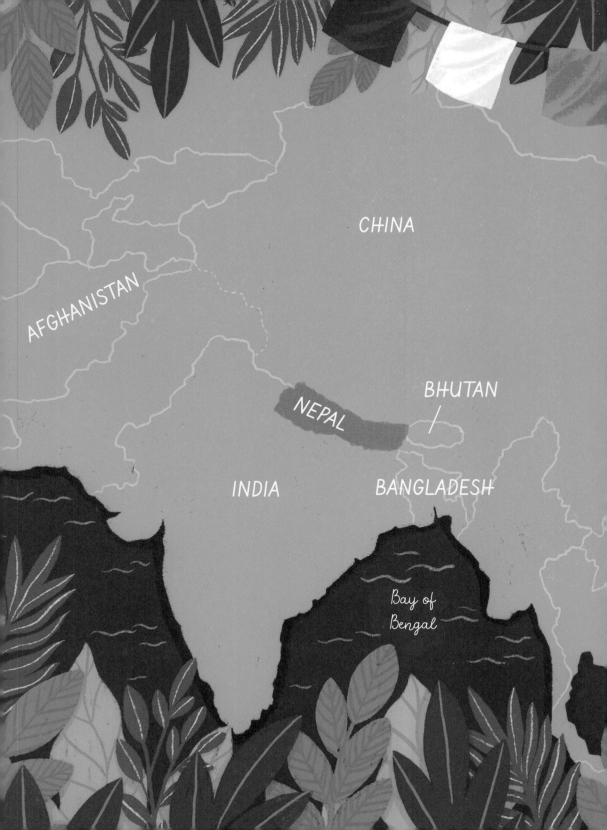

CHINA

AFGHANISTAN

NEPAL

BHUTAN

INDIA

BANGLADESH

Bay of
Bengal

KANEILA

NEPAL

NAMASTE.
My name is Kaneila.

कनेइला

KANEILA MEANS "BEAUTIFUL AS A ROSE."

I LIVE NEAR THE MOUNTAINS IN WESTERN NEPAL WITH MY MOTHER, MY BIG BROTHER AND MY LITTLE SISTER.

I live here, in the district of ACHHAM.

KATHMANDU, the capital city

Our village is so high up, our houses touch the clouds.

LIKE ALL THE OTHER VILLAGERS, MY FAMILY IS VERY RELIGIOUS. WE OFTEN GO TO THE TEMPLE TO PRAY AND BRING OFFERINGS TO THE GODS. THEY WILL PROTECT US, AND WE MUST THANK THEM.

THIS WEEK I'M GOING TO GET MY PERIOD. I WON'T BE ALLOWED TO GO TO THE TEMPLE. I WON'T BE ALLOWED TO GO TO SCHOOL EITHER.

I WON'T BE ALLOWED TO DO ANYTHING. ACCORDING TO THE TRADITIONAL PRACTICE OF CHHAUPADI, GIRLS WHO HAVE THEIR PERIOD ARE IMPURE AND ARE BANISHED FROM THE VILLAGE FOR A WEEK.

CHHAU

menstruation

PADI

woman

IN THE HINDU SCRIPTURES, IT IS
WRITTEN THAT MENSTRUAL BLOOD IS
THE PRODUCT OF A SIN PASSED DOWN
FROM THE GODS.

*dirty and
impure*

THE FIRST TIME I GOT MY PERIOD, I WAS USING THE BATHROOM
WHEN I SAW THE BLOOD. I PANICKED AND WENT TO SEE MY MOTHER.

"I'm bleeding.
I must be dying."

"You're a woman now.
You must sleep outside."

IF I TOUCH A COW, ITS MILK WILL DRY UP. IF I TOUCH ANY FOOD, FRUIT OR VEGETABLE, IT WILL ROT, AND IF I TOUCH A PLANT, ITS LEAVES WILL WILT. THAT'S WHY I MUST GO AND SLEEP IN THE CHHAU GOTH FOR SEVEN DAYS.

THE CHHAU GOTH IS A HUT FAR OUTSIDE THE VILLAGE. IT TAKES 20 MINUTES TO WALK THERE.

ONCE I GET THERE, MY MOTHER BLESSES THE HUT AND ASKS THE GODS FOR FORGIVENESS, AS IF GETTING MY PERIOD IS SOMETHING I'VE CHOSEN.

I BELIEVE IN THE GODS. I LOVE MY COUNTRY, MY VILLAGE, OUR TRADITIONS AND OUR CELEBRATIONS, BUT I DON'T LIKE CHHAUPADI. MORE AND MORE, I'M STARTING TO THINK THAT IT'S A SUPERSTITION.

MY MOTHER AND MY GRANDMOTHER DON'T LET ME SLEEP AT HOME. BEFORE NOW, I'VE NEVER ARGUED WITH THEM. I DIDN'T WANT ANYTHING BAD TO HAPPEN BECAUSE OF ME.

I LOVE PAPAYAS, BUT I'M NOT ALLOWED TO EAT OR EVEN TOUCH THEM WHEN I HAVE MY PERIOD. PAPAYAS ARE A SACRED FRUIT, AND IF I TOUCH ONE, THE WHOLE TREE WILL DIE.

ONE MORNING I PLUCKED UP THE COURAGE TO TOUCH A PAPAYA TO SEE IF THE FRUIT WOULD ROT OR THE TREE WOULD DIE.

I WAITED FOR A FEW DAYS, AND NOTHING HAPPENED.

NOW I'M CONVINCED CHHAUPADI IS SUPERSTITION, AND I DON'T BELIEVE IN IT ANYMORE.

IN THE DAYTIME PEOPLE BRING ME FOOD AND WATER, BUT THEY WON'T COME NEAR ME. TO WASH MYSELF, I MUST WALK FOR MILES TO A SPECIAL WELL BECAUSE I'M NOT ALLOWED TO TOUCH THE WATER IN THE VILLAGE. I MIGHT CONTAMINATE IT. WHEN I'M THERE, SOME PEOPLE WON'T EVEN SPEAK TO ME. I FEEL LIKE I'M INVISIBLE. UNTOUCHABLE.

EVERYONE HAS A STORY TO TELL TO JUSTIFY THIS TRADITION. ONCE A MAN EVEN TOLD ME HE LOST HIS SIGHT FOR A WEEK BECAUSE HE TOUCHED HIS DAUGHTER BY ACCIDENT WHEN SHE HAD HER PERIOD.

NIGHTTIME IS THE WORST. IT'S COLD OUTSIDE AND I'M SCARED OF THE WILD ANIMALS. RIGHT NOW IT'S THE RAINY SEASON, AND THERE ARE LOTS OF SNAKES. THE CHHAU GOTH HAS NO DOOR, SO ANYTHING—OR ANYONE— MIGHT COME IN. THERE'S NO WAY I CAN SLEEP TONIGHT. THE ANIMALS ARE NOT THE ONLY THREAT. SOME MEN HAVE NO RESPECT AND TAKE ADVANTAGE OF VULNERABLE GIRLS. I'M SCARED SOMEONE MIGHT COME IN. I'M TERRIFIED.

AS THE NIGHTS GO BY, MY FEAR TURNS TO ANGER.

TO END THIS WEEK OF BANISHMENT, I MUST BATHE AT THE CHHAUPADI DHARA.

TO PURIFY MYSELF.

ALSO, IF I TOUCH A BOOK WHILE I HAVE MY PERIOD, SARASVATI, THE GODDESS OF LEARNING, WILL UNLEASH HER ANGER ON ME.

I CAN GO BACK TO SCHOOL TODAY.

I LOVE BEING THERE. I LEARN A LOT AND I GET TO SEE MY FRIENDS.

DIRHA

IT'S A SPECIAL DAY. DIRHA'S COUSIN BIST HAS COME TO SPEAK TO OUR CLASS. SHE'S TRAVELED A LOT AND STUDIED BIOLOGY IN KATHMANDU. SHE COMES FROM A VILLAGE WHERE CHHAUPADI IS NO LONGER PRACTICED.

DIRHA'S FAMILY DOESN'T SEND HER TO THE CHHAU GOTH WHEN SHE HAS HER PERIOD. INSTEAD, SHE SLEEPS IN A SEPARATE ROOM CALLED A BAITKAK.

SHE TELLS US THAT TWO GIRLS WERE BITTEN TO DEATH BY A SNAKE IN THE CHHAU GOTH.

THE WOMEN IN THEIR VILLAGE REALIZED THAT THE GODS HAD NOTHING TO DO WITH THE PRACTICE OF BANISHING GIRLS. THEY HAD OBEYED THE TRADITION, BUT THE GODS DIDN'T PROTECT THE GIRLS. AND SO THE WOMEN DECIDED TO ABANDON THE TRADITION, EVEN THOUGH IT MADE THE PRIESTS AND SOME OF THE VILLAGERS ANGRY.

BIST EXPLAINS TO THE CLASS HOW MENSTRUATION WORKS. WE'RE ALL VERY INTERESTED. BUT WE'RE A LITTLE EMBARRASSED, TOO, BECAUSE NOBODY HAS EVER TOLD US THIS BEFORE, ESPECIALLY IN FRONT OF BOYS.

SOME PEOPLE IN CLASS ARE SO EMBARRASSED, THEY LEAVE THE ROOM.

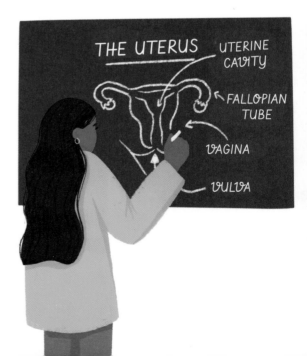

THE UTERUS

UTERINE CAVITY

FALLOPIAN TUBE

VAGINA

VULVA

I'M FASCINATED BY EVERYTHING BIST TELLS US. SHE SAYS SHE'LL COME AND TALK TO OUR FAMILIES IF WE LIKE.

UNTIL NOW I'VE ALWAYS THOUGHT THE GODS WERE PUNISHING ME FOR BEING BORN A GIRL. I USED TO THINK I WAS DIRTY. I USED TO FEEL HUMILIATED WHEN I HAD MY PERIOD. BUT NOW I KNOW THAT MENSTRUATION IS NATURAL FOR WOMEN ALL OVER THE WORLD. IF WOMEN IN BIST'S VILLAGE HAVE STOPPED OBEYING CHHAUPADI, WHY CAN'T WE?

Periods are nothing to be ashamed of.

OUR FAMILIES LOVE US. THEY MAKE US OBEY CHHAUPADI BECAUSE THEY THINK IT'S THE RIGHT THING TO DO. MAYBE THEY'LL SEE THAT IT ISN'T IF WE TELL THEM THE STORY OF THOSE TWO GIRLS WHO DIED IN THE CHHAU GOTH AND EXPLAIN HOW NATURAL PERIODS ARE.

MY MOTHER DOESN'T LIKE CHHAUPADI EITHER. SHE OBEYS IT OUT OF TRADITION AND ESPECIALLY FEAR. I THINK THAT ONE DAY SHE'LL UNDERSTAND.

LOTS OF WOMEN DON'T LIKE CHHAUPADI, BUT THEY DON'T TALK ABOUT IT. THEY'RE AFRAID OF WHAT OTHERS MIGHT THINK. BUT IF WE TALKED OPENLY ABOUT IT, WE COULD CHANGE THE TRADITION.

NOW I WANT TO STUDY TO BECOME A TEACHER, TO MAKE SURE THAT GIRLS ARE SAFE FROM DANGER AND NEVER HAVE TO FEEL ASHAMED OF THEIR PERIODS AND THEIR BODIES AGAIN.

Today I have hope. I'm sure that things will change!

WHAT'S THE STORY BEHIND CHHAUPADI?

In Hindu mythology, Indra was urged by Vishnu, the god of time, to commit a terrible sin by killing a Brahmin, who was a very important man. Indra was cursed and hid himself inside a flower for a whole year, hoping to be forgiven for his sin.

The story might have ended there, but Indra, again urged by Vishnu, decided to divide his sin and share it with the trees, the earth, the water and—guess who?—women! When Indra passed on a part of his sin to women, he created menstruation and made them bleed every month. This was how periods came to be thought of as dirty and sinful. Ever since then, women have been considered impure when they are menstruating, and anyone who comes near them will also be cursed.

The Hindu religion is based on a number of stories and myths. There are rituals to worship many gods. One of the festivals celebrated by Hindus every year is Rishi Panchami, and its history is connected to menstruation. Women traditionally go to sacred rivers and perform rituals to purify themselves of sins they may have committed while menstruating.

Menstruation is often associated with sin in myths and religious texts. This has fed people's beliefs and superstitions and made menstruation a taboo subject. Chhaupadi is a clear example of a dangerous practice that originated with a myth and became a centuries-old tradition that overshadowed the science of menstruation and women's bodies.

THIS IS THE BEST HIDING PLACE!

ONLY 364 DAYS TO GO.

WHAT'S A TABOO?

A *taboo* is something people don't talk about, often because of awkwardness or shame. The subject may be something intimate and personal, or it may be something to do with religion or family. It's the kind of thing we aren't supposed to discuss with other people.

When a subject becomes taboo, it becomes untouchable, and that's a problem. People pretend it doesn't exist, even if it's a huge, awkward thing like an elephant in the room. Because menstruation is seen as too personal a topic to talk about, we have come to think of it as shameful and taboo—even though it's something that every person with a uterus will likely experience!

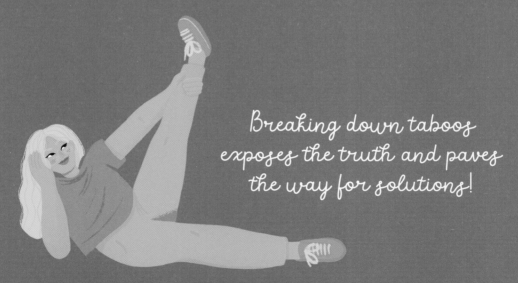

Breaking down taboos exposes the truth and paves the way for solutions!

SERIOUSLY, WHAT'S THE POINT OF PERIODS?

Periods are nothing to be ashamed of. They're actually pretty amazing. When you think about it, the body can do some awesome things. It's good to remind ourselves of that sometimes.

The menstrual cycle lasts about 28 days, depending on the individual. The cycle begins on the first day of the period and ends on the first day of the next period. It's regulated by hormones in the brain. Halfway through the cycle, an egg is released from an ovary. The egg then travels down the fallopian tube into the uterus.

abracadabra

I have the magic power to create life.

And every month the uterus prepares a cozy little nest just in case an egg gets fertilized by a sperm. It does this by thickening the endometrium, which is the tissue that lines the uterus. If the egg is not fertilized, the nest is not needed. So the uterus sheds the excess blood and tissue, and that's the stuff that ends up in your underwear. That's your period. Menstrual bleeding can last between three and seven days. The cycle repeats itself every month.

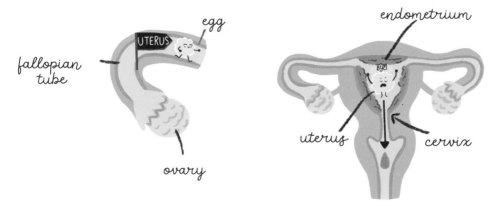

fallopian tube

UTERUS

egg

ovary

endometrium

uterus

cervix

BREAKING THE TABOO, PERIOD

For too many girls around the world, menstruation is a sign to their families that they are old enough to marry and bear children. Beliefs like this are responsible for thousands of dangerous early pregnancies. Most girls get their first period when they are between 10 and 14 years old, but that doesn't mean they immediately become women who are ready to have children of their own. They still have a lot of growing up to do.

In Nepal, 37 percent of girls are married before the age of 18, even though the minimum legal age is 20. Poverty, lack of access to education, tradition and social pressures are often to blame. Unfortunately, that's also the case in many other countries.

These inequalities are passed down from one generation to the next. But girls should not have to keep living in danger and in shame every month.

Traditions can be hard to break. And they don't disappear overnight. Believe it or not, it's not necessarily men who make girls and young women obey chhaupadi. Much of the time it's older women who keep the tradition going, partly because of guilt and shame and mostly due to lack of information. They

would rather force the younger generation into menstrual exile than live in fear of something bad happening because they didn't.

In 2005 the Supreme Court of Nepal passed a law prohibiting anyone from forcing women to practice chhaupadi. Many villages have now torn down their chhau goths to symbolize their emancipation.

PERIODS ARE NOT JUST A "GIRL THING"

No matter where in the world we look, the same kinds of issues tend to come up when we talk about periods. These issues are related to health, education, poverty and shame. If we don't teach people about menstruation, it's like pretending periods don't exist. It's important for everyone to have this knowledge.

Yes, everyone! Not just girls. At school, boys often think periods are none of their business. There's no reason why they can't talk to their friends about periods. They can listen, take action and do their part to stop the mocking. Teachers who care about these issues can also play an important role. Students who are aware can be empowered to speak up and take action against inequality, which can help to ease the burden on women's lives and ultimately change the world. So periods are not just a personal thing and not just a girl thing. Periods are political!

On average, a person will have her period for 2,555 days over the course of her life. How are women supposed to build self-confidence and dare to express themselves if all they can think about every month is making themselves small and coping with the bleeding and the pain?

You just don't get it, do you? There's nothing funny about periods, and you're just making them more taboo!

PERIODS COST MONEY

When you have your period, you have to use menstrual products such as pads or tampons every day. Even today, all around the world, many women must choose between buying period protection and putting food on the table. There's a name for this dilemma. Period poverty affects as many as 500 million women. There's more to it than just struggling to afford menstrual protection. Many women don't even have access to clean running water to wash themselves during their period.

Some women in developing countries use sand, dead leaves or ashes for protection. Some hide their stained rags under their mattress or in the roofs of the huts they are banished to, or they burn them in secret. They're too embarrassed to wash them or hang them to dry where others might see them. This can lead to infection and potentially fatal illnesses. Menstruation is the main reason why girls miss school in developing countries. Being excluded makes them ashamed of their bodies and subjects them to inequality and injustice. And it puts their health and their lives at risk.

All women have a right to dignity. Periods should never deprive them of that.

A NEW TIME FOR PERIODS!

In Nepal and India, as well as in some parts of Africa, women's groups and associations are campaigning against period poverty and the menstruation taboo. They've been teaching people how to sew pads that are washable and reusable, and knocking on doors to raise awareness about menstruation and hygiene, all to help prevent menstrual exile for girls in the future.

These initiatives demand commitment and courage. Some people and governments are opposed to these campaigns. They are afraid of women becoming empowered. In some countries in Southeast Asia, women who have painful periods are granted menstrual leave so they can rest. Other countries are thinking about implementing this too. It's a good idea, but the problem is, in a sexist world this can also be a pretext to hire fewer women, pay them less than men or sideline them because they are "impure." In other words, the fight is far from over.

In 2020 Scotland became the first country to provide free menstrual products to any person who needs them. This is an example for other countries to follow. In some countries, pads and tampons are distributed in schools and other public places. Now that's a step in the right direction!

UNITED KINGDOM

GERMANY

BELGIUM

English Channel

FRANCE

SWITZERLAND

Atlantic Ocean

ITALY

SPAIN

Mediterranean
Sea

JADE

FRANCE

BONJOUR!
My name is Jade.

JADE

I HAVE THE SAME NAME AS A GREEN GEMSTONE THAT'S SUPPOSED TO SOOTHE THE BODY AND MIND.

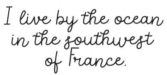

I live by the ocean in the southwest of France.

PARIS, the capital city

I LIVE WITH MY PARENTS AND MY BIG SISTER.

I can see the blue of the ocean from my window.
A few times a week, I take my dog, Poppy,
for a walk on the beach.

I SPEND A LOT OF TIME IN MY ROOM, ON MY LAPTOP. I LISTEN TO MUSIC. I WATCH VIDEOS. BUT I REALLY LIKE TO WRITE AND DRAW.

MY SISTER, ADÈLE, AND I ARE VERY CLOSE. SHE COMES TO MY ROOM TO SEE ME A LOT. AND SHE ALWAYS INVITES ME ALONG WHEN SHE GOES OUT.

How can you be a size XL already, at your age?

What a shame! You have such a pretty face.

I HAVE A COMPLICATED RELATIONSHIP WITH MY MOTHER. SOMETIMES I THINK ALL SHE CARES ABOUT IS HER WORK AND HER APPEARANCE. AND MINE TOO—MOSTLY MINE.

SHE COMPARES ME TO MY SISTER. A LOT.

I TRY NOT TO LET IT BOTHER ME, BUT THE THINGS SHE SAYS MAKE ME SAD, AND SOMETIMES I GET MAD AT HER. EVEN WHEN I'M TRYING MY BEST, I ALWAYS FEEL LIKE I'M NOT GOOD ENOUGH. ADÈLE IS THE ONLY PERSON WHO ENCOURAGES ME. SHE SAYS A LOT OF NICE THINGS TO ME.

You're awesome. You're funny and you're creative. You can do anything!

MY MOTHER ISN'T THE ONLY ONE WHO SAYS THINGS THAT HURT. PEOPLE AT SCHOOL HAVE MADE JOKES ABOUT ME AND SAID UNKIND THINGS.

Come on, Jade, put some effort into it!

THE GYM TEACHER THINKS I SHOULD WORK HARDER THAN EVERYONE ELSE.

PLUS, SOME BOYS KEEP SAYING THERE'S NO WAY THEY'D EVER WANT TO BE WITH ME. IT'S NOT LIKE I WAS EVEN ASKING THEM!

ONE DAY I HAD A FEVER, SO MY MOTHER TOOK ME TO
THE DOCTOR'S OFFICE. AS SOON AS I STEPPED ON THE
SCALE, ALL THE DOCTOR WANTED TO TALK ABOUT WAS
MY WEIGHT.

AND YOU KNOW
WHAT HE SAID
TO ME?

*A pretty girl like you shouldn't
let herself go like this.*

I DON'T THINK HE MEANT ANY HARM, BUT I
WAS HUMILIATED.

WHEN WE GOT HOME, MY MOTHER PUT ME
ON A STRICT DIET. SHE EVEN HID FOOD
FROM ME!

NOW SHE KEEPS SAYING THE SAME THINGS,
OVER AND OVER.

*"No more carbs and no more
sugar! Eat smaller portions."*

"You should skip dessert."

"Careful—some vegetables are high in calories."

SHE WEIGHS THE FOOD ON MY PLATE.

NOW I DON'T EAT THE SAME THING AS EVERYONE ELSE. EVERYTHING IS STEAMED. MY MOTHER CONTROLS EVERYTHING I DO. I'M THE ODD ONE OUT IN THE FAMILY.

ENJOY!

SOUP. AGAIN.

I CAN SEE THAT MY FATHER FEELS AWKWARD.

NOW I CAN'T STOP THINKING ABOUT THINGS PEOPLE HAVE SAID TO ME ABOUT MY WEIGHT SINCE I WAS A KID.

IT'S FUNNY HOW EVERYONE'S ALWAYS HAD AN OPINION ABOUT MY BODY AND A THEORY ABOUT MY WEIGHT. EVERYONE SEEMS TO THINK THEY'RE AN EXPERT IN NUTRITION.

IT'S NOT AS IF I EVER ASKED THEM TO TELL ME WHAT THEY THINK.

I HAVE TO WEIGH MYSELF SEVERAL TIMES A WEEK. THAT'S ALL I EVER THINK ABOUT NOW. I DON'T EVEN WANT TO LOOK AT THE NUMBER ON THE SCALE.

I JUST HOPE IT WILL GO DOWN SO PEOPLE WILL GIVE ME A BREAK.

WHEN I LOSE OUNCES, IT'S A SMALL VICTORY. WHEN I LOSE POUNDS, EVERYONE CONGRATULATES ME.

BUT IT'S STILL NOT
ENOUGH.

AND I FEEL LIKE IT
NEVER WILL BE.

I DON'T EVEN FEEL LIKE WRITING OR DRAWING ANYMORE. I'M HUNGRY, AND I CAN'T HANDLE ALL THE PRESSURE. I WISH I COULD DISAPPEAR. THAT WAY PEOPLE WOULD JUST LEAVE ME ALONE.

BUT ALL THEY SEE IS ME. EVEN WHEN I DON'T SAY ANYTHING ABOUT IT, MY BODY IS THE CENTER OF ATTENTION. PEOPLE TALK ABOUT IT AS IF I SHOULD BE OKAY WITH EVERYTHING.

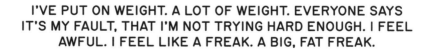

I'VE PUT ON WEIGHT. A LOT OF WEIGHT. EVERYONE SAYS IT'S MY FAULT, THAT I'M NOT TRYING HARD ENOUGH. I FEEL AWFUL. I FEEL LIKE A FREAK. A BIG, FAT FREAK.

I KNOW I'M NOT IN A GOOD PLACE RIGHT NOW. I DON'T WANT TO GET OUT OF BED. I'M SPENDING ALL MY TIME ON MY PHONE.

IF ONLY I COULD LOOK LIKE ALL THESE GIRLS. THEY SEEM SO HAPPY!

JULIA.QUITESIMPLY

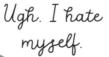

Ugh. I hate myself.

MY SISTER TELLS ME TO FORGET ABOUT DIETING AND NOT TO WORRY ABOUT MY WEIGHT. WHAT'S REALLY IMPORTANT IS FOR ME TO FEEL GOOD ABOUT MYSELF AGAIN.

I KNOW SHE'S RIGHT, BUT I CAN'T GET ALL THAT STUFF OUT OF MY HEAD.

MY BEST FRIEND, CLARA, CAME AND TALKED TO ME TODAY. SHE TOLD ME I'VE CHANGED. SHE SAID I DON'T LAUGH LIKE I USED TO.

I DECIDED TO OPEN UP TO HER. I TOLD HER HOW HARD ALL OF THIS FEELS FOR ME. I TOLD HER HOW YUCKY AND UNCOMFORTABLE I FEEL IN MY BODY.

SHE SAID WE DON'T HAVE TO LIVE UP TO OTHER PEOPLE'S EXPECTATIONS. EVER SINCE SHE WAS SMALL, SHE'S BEEN TEASED ABOUT WHERE SHE'S FROM. THAT MAKES HER ANGRY. SHE TRIES TO CHEER ME UP.

"You can be proud to be you!"
"Don't ruin your life for something you can't change!
You are what you are."

YOUR BODY IS AMAZING. LOOK AT ALL THE THINGS YOU CAN DO WITH IT!

I can sit and enjoy the view.

I can laugh until I cry.

I can fall in love.

I can feel the sun on my skin.

I can walk on the beach.

I can enjoy good food.

I can swim.

I can dance.

CLARA'S KNOWN ME SINCE I WAS LITTLE. I KNOW SHE'S RIGHT.

I WORKED UP THE COURAGE TO
WRITE MY PARENTS A LETTER TO
TELL THEM I FIND THE PRESSURE
OF DIETING TOO HARD. IT'S TOO
MUCH FOR ME TO DO.

THEY CAME TO TALK TO ME RIGHT
AWAY. MY MOTHER WAS WORRIED.

"I DIDN'T REALIZE HOW
MISERABLE THE DIETING
WAS MAKING YOU FEEL!"
MY FATHER JUST CRIED
AND TOLD ME HOW MUCH
THEY BOTH LOVE ME.
HE COULDN'T BELIEVE
I'D BEEN HAVING SUCH
NEGATIVE THOUGHTS
ABOUT MYSELF. HE
DOESN'T EXPRESS HIS
FEELINGS VERY OFTEN,
BUT NOW I KNOW I CAN
COUNT ON HIM.

IT'S DECIDED. THERE'S NO MORE DIETING. FROM NOW ON WE'RE GOING
TO KEEP AN EYE ON MY OVERALL HEALTH AND NOT JUST MY WEIGHT.

THIS WHOLE EXPERIENCE HAS GIVEN ME AN IDEA!

I REACH FOR MY SKETCHBOOK AGAIN, AND I START WRITING. MY HEROINE IS GOING TO BE CURVY. SHE'S GOING TO HAVE A BODY LIKE MINE!

WOW! LOOK HOW STRONG SHE IS!

SHE'S SO COOL!

I CAN MAKE HER SO AWESOME, NO ONE WILL CARE WHAT PANT SIZE SHE WEARS. IT WON'T EVEN BE TALKED ABOUT, BECAUSE REALLY, IT'S NO ONE ELSE'S BUSINESS.

FROM NOW ON I'M NOT TAKING ORDERS FROM ANYONE. I'M NOT JUST GOING TO SMILE POLITELY ANYMORE AT PEOPLE WHO MAKE COMMENTS AND JOKES ABOUT MY BODY.

I'M SICK OF BEING JUDGED FOR IT. I AM SO MUCH MORE THAN A BODY.

I AM CARING.

I LOVE POPPY.

I LOVE LIVING CLOSE TO NATURE.

I AM CREATIVE.

I AM SENSITIVE.

I LOVE MY FAMILY.

I LOVE MY FRIENDS.

I AM KIND.

WHAT'S THE POINT IN CHANGING MY APPEARANCE TO PLEASE OTHER PEOPLE? AND TO PLEASE WHOM, EXACTLY?

I'VE REALIZED THAT PRETTY MUCH EVERYONE GETS JUDGED ABOUT STUPID THINGS. AND LOTS OF MY FRIENDS HAVE BEEN TEASED ABOUT THINGS BEFORE. I CAN'T HELP BUT THINK THAT, NO MATTER WHAT WE DO, WE'LL NEVER BE PERFECT.

THE MOST IMPORTANT THING IS FOR ME TO FEEL GOOD ABOUT MYSELF. THAT DOESN'T MEAN IT WON'T BE HARD SOMETIMES FOR ME TO EMBRACE AND APPRECIATE THE BODY I'M IN. BUT THAT'S MY BUSINESS AND NOBODY ELSE'S!

WHO SAYS GIRLS HAVE TO BE PRETTY?

Society's standards tend to be sexist and very hard on women. All too often women are judged on their appearance and made to feel that they have to be pretty to be valued. Many women are influenced by these societal pressures and subconsciously imitate the "ideal" models they see on social media and elsewhere—to the point of obsession.

Would any girl who found herself alone on a desert island care about her weight or have any desire to shave her body hair and cover up her zits? No, of course not!

In our consumer society, diet and cosmetics companies are making big profits. Brands use different strategies to encourage women to diet and be slim. Some even try to persuade women that injections or surgery are the way to achieve "natural" beauty. They're trying to control the female body and sell the ideal of perfect beauty and eternal youth. In a truly ideal world, where every woman felt good about her body, this industry would collapse!

In the 19th century, Empress Elisabeth of Austria was obsessed with her beauty and spent her life trying to maintain it. She was known for her rivalry with Empress Eugénie. She wanted to be the one with the best figure and the longest hair. She wanted to stay young forever. Her obsession drove her to starve herself and exercise too much. She even used to hide her face as she grew old.

The quest for beauty also encourages women to see each other as rivals. And this makes the fight for women's rights even more important!

I'M FREEEE!

WHAT'S THE POINT OF IT ALL?

When girls see only role models with slim bodies, they think the worst thing that can happen to them is to gain weight. Fifty-four percent of girls ages 14 to 17 have been subjected to anti-fat comments and behavior. As early as age 6, some girls express concerns about their weight. And around half of all girls between the ages of 6 and 12 are worried about gaining weight.

Unfortunately, these unrealistic ideals can stay with us for life. And the consequences can be disastrous. Some of us will develop an eating disorder, such as anorexia nervosa. This is especially common in girls and young women between the ages of 12 and 20. Girls are much more likely to develop this disorder than boys are. Here in North America, the number of hospitalizations has risen sharply in just one generation. This cult of thinness, which focuses so much on our weight and what we eat, can put our physical and mental health at risk. Good health is not about weight alone. We should focus on other indicators instead, especially when it comes to protecting our mental health.

Thirty-seven percent of 11-year-old girls say they are dieting or have been on a diet.

JUST THE WAY YOU ARE

What's the big deal about girls being big? The body-positivity movement has emerged in response to this kind of pressure and criticism. It encourages us to celebrate the diversity of bodies out there and accept ourselves the way we are. But the body-positivity movement has a downside—the plus-size models we see might wear XL clothes, but they're usually shapely women with big boobs, broad hips and a slimmer waist. They may be bigger, but their full figures still reflect the desirable body ideal that society considers acceptable. Basically, these "positive" body representations have just created a new norm. Not only that, but body positivity can also make women feel extra pressure to love their bodies no matter what.

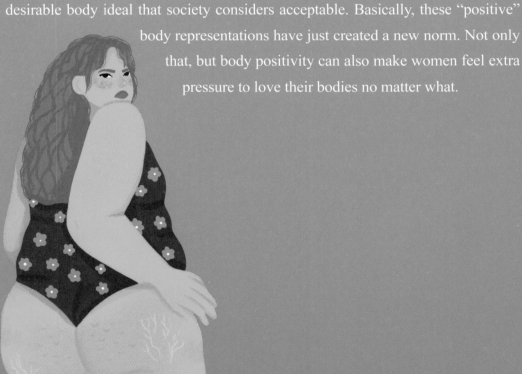

TOO SHORT.
TAKE CARE OF YOUR SKIN!
NOT FEMININE ENOUGH.
TOO TALL.
STRAIGHTEN YOUR HAIR! STYLE YOUR HAIR!
TOO SKINNY! EAT MORE!
JUST SHAVE, WILL YOU! BODY HAIR IS GROSS!

TOO FLAT-CHESTED.

TOO COVERED-UP!

BE MORE
NATURAL.

SHE'S JUST
ASKING FOR IT.

TRASHY.
PUT A
BRA ON!

IS THAT A GUY OR A GIRL?

STOP!

WHO ARE OUR HEROINES?

Every day we're bombarded with thousands of images. Videos, ads, magazines and movies all expose us to things that shape our imaginations. From an early age, children identify with the fictional characters they see. It's important to make sure they see role models who look like regular people, not just stereotypes.

In the movies a lot of female roles are written to appeal to a heterosexual male audience. Often a female character's actions are secondary to what she looks like, or she's only on-screen to make the hero look irresistible. There's a name for this way of objectifying women. It's called the *male gaze*. In many movie scenes, the camerawork and the esthetic choices are all about showing women as objects of desire. When the camera zooms in on a woman's behind, chances are it's not to enhance the story line. When sexy equals successful on-screen, it sends a message to women in the audience that they should look and behave the same way. And that's a problem for anyone with a body that doesn't check the stereotypical beauty boxes.

Can you think of any movies that feature a plus-size female character and a story line that doesn't revolve around her hang-ups or a change in her body? The industry is trying, but most movies are still produced and directed by men. The female gaze promises to bring a new perspective to the movies and change our experience as moviegoers.

YESSSS REVOLUTION!

The Bechdel Test

THIS IS A WAY TO MEASURE THE
REPRESENTATION OF WOMEN IN MOVIES.

1

DOES THE MOVIE HAVE AT LEAST
TWO WOMEN IN IT WHO ARE NAMED?

Petunia

Hortense

2

DO THESE TWO WOMEN
TALK TO EACH OTHER?

*DID YOU SEE
THE CAFETERIA
HAS FRIES ON THE
MENU TODAY?*

3

DO THEY TALK ABOUT
SOMETHING OTHER
THAN A MAN?

IT'S CRAZY, BUT THIS REALLY IS THE BARE MINIMUM.
AROUND FOUR OUT OF TEN MOVIES FAIL THE TEST.

＊ *RESULTS OF VIEWING 4,000 FILMS.*

JUST GIVE US A BREAK!

Our bodies change over the course of our lives. There are just as many reasons for being overweight or underweight as there are individual people. We all have our own story, and it's nobody's business but our own. It's time for us to think of others as people, without letting gender and body shape color our gaze and our judgment.

One step in the right direction is the I Weigh movement, an initiative started by Jameela Jamil to create a safe and inclusive space on social media. This caring community shifts the focus to people's qualities, rather than their weight. So instead of saying how many pounds (kilograms) someone's carrying, you might instead "weigh" the awesomeness of their family, their caring attitude or their optimism. When it comes to attraction, it's normal to have preferences, but we shouldn't forget that our gaze is shaped by society. For example, if you're attracted to tall, dark, handsome guys with a square jaw, that might be because you've seen a lot of images of people with those features.

There's a whole system in society that influences how we perceive others, and people are often discriminated against solely on the basis of how they look. Some are more respected and privileged than others. This doesn't necessarily mean life is easy for them, but they might never have to face racism or sexism, and that gives them a certain amount of power. It's good for them to be aware of this so they can use their privilege to help others!

safe space

LIKED BY 2,697 PEOPLE WHO CARE.
YAY FOR THE POSITIVE
POWER OF SOCIAL MEDIA!

UZBEKISTAN

TURKMENISTAN

TAJIKISTAN

IRAN

AFGHANISTAN

PAKISTAN

NEPAL

INDIA

Arabian Sea

MAHNOOSH

AFGHANISTAN

SALAM!

My name is Mahnoosh.

ماهنش

MAHNOOSH MEANS "MOONLIGHT" IN PERSIAN.

I'm from KANDAHAR, in Afghanistan.

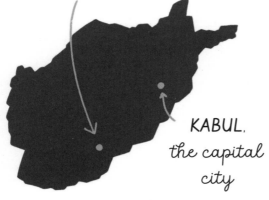

KABUL, the capital city

I LIVE WITH MY FATHER, MY MOTHER AND MY SIX SISTERS.

Our mud houses are like mazes.
It gets very hot here in summer.

"*Cover up and keep quiet.*"

HERE, IF YOU'RE BORN A GIRL, YOU'RE DESTINED FOR A VERY DIFFERENT LIFE.

"*I'm so proud of you, my son!*"

IT'S VERY IMPORTANT FOR EVERY FAMILY TO HAVE A SON. A SON IS SEEN AS A BLESSING BECAUSE A BOY CAN HELP A FAMILY EARN MONEY. WITHOUT A SON, A FAMILY IS VULNERABLE AND INCOMPLETE.

I WAS BORN A GIRL. IT'S A CURSE THAT FORCES ME INTO A LIFE WITHOUT FREEDOM.

But I have a secret.

I'M NOT A REGULAR KIND OF GIRL. I'M
A BACHA POSH. IN DARI, THAT MEANS
"DRESSED LIKE A BOY."

IN THE DAYTIME I BECOME A BOY, AND
MY NAME IS MAHYAR. MAHYAR MEANS
"FRIEND OF THE MOON." AND AT THE
END OF THE DAY, AT HOME, I BECOME
MAHNOOSH AGAIN.

EVERY MORNING I DRESS IN BOYS' CLOTHING TO HELP MY FATHER IN HIS STORE. THIS WAS THE ONLY WAY I COULD WORK THERE.

THE ONLY PERSON WE'VE TOLD IS MY UNCLE AYDIN. IF ANYONE ELSE FINDS OUT, THEY'LL REPORT US TO THE TALIBAN.

MY UNCLE AYDIN

THESE MEN ARE ARMED. THEY CONTROL EVERYTHING. THEIR RULES ARE VERY STRICT.

BEING A BACHA POSH GIVES ME MORE FREEDOM.
WHEN I LOOK AT MY BIG SISTERS, I CAN SEE WHAT MY LIFE WILL BE LIKE
LATER. THEY HELP OUR MOTHER AT HOME AND WILL GET MARRIED SOON.

MY LITTLE SISTERS WERE
LUCKY. THEY WERE ABLE TO GO
TO SCHOOL FOR A WHILE. BUT
NOW THEY'RE NOT ALLOWED.

THE TALIBAN RULES THE WHOLE
COUNTRY. SOME PEOPLE HAVE FLED
THE COUNTRY. THEY'RE THE LUCKY
ONES. OTHERS DARE TO RESIST.
MY SISTERS ARE AFRAID TO
GO OUTSIDE. MY PARENTS ARE
WORRIED TOO. THEY'RE TIRED OF
THE WAR. THEY'RE SCARED OF
LOSING ONE OF THEIR DAUGHTERS.

IT'S A NIGHTMARE FOR A FAMILY TO
HAVE SEVEN DAUGHTERS.

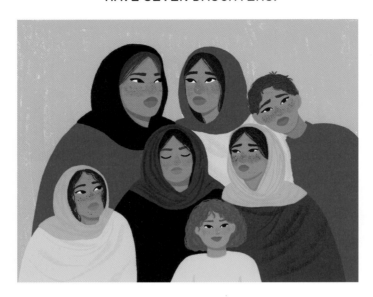

WHEN MY MOTHER WAS EXPECTING HER THIRD CHILD,
SHE WAS SURE IT WAS GOING TO BE A BOY THAT TIME.

"Please, not another girl."

SHE PREPARED EVERYTHING
FOR MY ARRIVAL. SHE BOUGHT
CLOTHES FOR A BABY BOY. SHE
WAS SO PROUD TO BE HAVING A
SON! THAT'S PROBABLY WHY MY
PARENTS DECIDED TO MAKE ME
A BACHA POSH.

A WOMAN WHO CAN'T GIVE BIRTH TO A BABY BOY IS CALLED A *SANDA* OR A *KHOSHK*. THOSE ARE THE WORDS FOR "BARREN" OR "DRY" IN DARI.

PEOPLE EVEN SAY THAT IF A WOMAN HAS NO SON, SHE SHOULD HAVE TRIED HARDER AND WANTED A BOY MORE BADLY. SOMEHOW IT'S ALWAYS HER FAULT IF SHE DOESN'T HAVE A SON!

MY FATHER TOOK ME OUT OF SCHOOL
WHEN I WAS SEVEN YEARS OLD. HE SAID
IT WAS A WASTE OF TIME! THAT WAS
WHEN HE ASKED ME IF I WANTED TO
BECOME A BOY.

Do I want to be able to walk around without
someone telling me what to do?
Do I want to be free?
OF COURSE!

MY MOTHER CUT MY HAIR. I
STARTED TO DRESS LIKE A BOY.
I STARTED A NEW LIFE.

WHEN GIRLS REACH ADOLESCENCE, THINGS CHANGE QUICKLY. MARRIAGE PROPOSALS START ROLLING IN. THERE'S A PERSIAN EXPRESSION ABOUT GIRLS AND BOYS:

"A SON BELONGS TO THE FAMILY AND A DAUGHTER BELONGS TO ALL."

FOR NOW, AT LEAST, I CAN RUN AROUND, I CAN FLY A KITE, I CAN PLAY OUTSIDE, AND I CAN PLAY SPORTS. MY SISTERS COULD NEVER DO ANY OF THIS. IT WOULD BE DISHONORABLE!

SOMETIMES I FORGET I'M A GIRL. I CAN WALK DOWN THE STREET AND HOLD MY HEAD HIGH. I CAN DO WHAT I WANT! I HAVE MORE FREEDOM THAN MY MOTHER DOES.

THE STREETS BELONG TO MEN. AND THE LAWS
MADE BY THE TALIBAN SAY THAT WOMEN MUST
BE COVERED FROM HEAD TO TOE. LIKE THEY'RE
INVISIBLE. THOSE WHO ONCE DARED TO SHOW
THEIR FACES HAVE TO COVER THEM WITH DARK
VEILS TO HIDE THEIR EYES AND THEIR MOUTHS.
THEY CAN'T GO OUT ALONE ANYMORE.

IT'S NOT EASY WORKING WITH MY FATHER. I HAVE TO CARRY HEAVY THINGS. IT'S EXHAUSTING BEING OUT IN THE SUN AND THE WIND AND THE DUST.

I PREFER HELPING MY UNCLE AYDIN. HE'S THE ONLY ONE IN OUR FAMILY WHO'S BEEN TO COLLEGE, AND HE DOESN'T THINK LIKE OTHER MEN.

MY FATHER DOESN'T LIKE TO DRAW ATTENTION TO HIMSELF. HE WANTS US TO KEEP OUR HEADS DOWN TO AVOID ANY TROUBLE.

MY FATHER

ME

THE ONLY PHOTO ON THE WALL AT HOME.

STILL, HE TAKES A RISK WHEN HE BRINGS ME ALONG TO PRAYERS AT THE MOSQUE. MEN AND WOMEN AREN'T ALLOWED TO PRAY TOGETHER.

I LIKE GOING THERE WITH HIM, BECAUSE IT'S THE ONLY SPECIAL QUIET TIME WE GET TO SHARE TOGETHER.

Sometimes I don't really know who I am anymore or how I should act.

MAHYAR OR MAHNOOSH?

WHEN A BACHA POSH REACHES PUBERTY, THEY CAN'T LIVE AS A BOY ANY LONGER. IT'S NOT ACCEPTABLE. I KNOW WHAT THAT MEANS.

IT MEANS SAYING GOODBYE TO MY DREAMS AND MY DAY-TO-DAY LIFE. IT MEANS BECOMING A WIFE, THEN A MOTHER. IT MEANS COVERING MY HAIR AND KEEPING MY MOUTH SHUT.

NO WAY!

I WANT TO FEEL THE WIND IN MY HAIR. I WANT MY VOICE TO BE HEARD AS MUCH AS A BOY'S. NOW THAT I'VE GROWN UP THIS WAY, I CAN'T JUST BITE MY TONGUE. I DON'T WANT TO BE LIKE A BIRD IN A CAGE.

I'M HELPING MY UNCLE WITH HIS WORK ONE EVENING WHEN SUDDENLY MY FATHER COMES IN. HE TAKES MY UNCLE ASIDE TO TALK TO HIM. I CAN HEAR THEM ARGUING. THEY KEEP SAYING MY NAME. THEY OBVIOUSLY DON'T AGREE ABOUT SOMETHING, AND IT'S SOMETHING TO DO WITH ME. WHEN THEY'RE DONE, MY FATHER IS IN A HURRY TO TAKE ME HOME.

NOW MY PARENTS SEEM UNCOMFORTABLE EVERY TIME SOMEONE MENTIONS MY NAME. THEY KNOW I DON'T WANT TO GIVE UP MY LIFE AS A BACHA POSH.

THEY WANT ME TO ACT "LIKE A GIRL."

WHO WANTS TO DO THAT IF IT MEANS STAYING AT HOME AND KEEPING YOUR MOUTH SHUT? MY LITTLE SISTERS AND I HAVE ALL BEEN TO SCHOOL. WE LONG FOR A DIFFERENT LIFE.

ONE DAY I HOPE I CAN BE INDEPENDENT AND HAVE A JOB OF MY OWN. BUT HOW CAN I DREAM OF THAT WHEN I SEE GIRLS LOCKED UP AT HOME? MY ONLY HOPE IS TO KEEP ON BEING A BACHA POSH.

ONCE WHEN OUR MOTHER IS BUSY, ONE OF MY LITTLE SISTERS TELLS US ABOUT SOME GIRLS WHO MEET IN SECRET IN A BASEMENT. THEY'RE LEARNING HOW TO FIGHT.

I TELL MY SISTERS THAT I CAN GO ALONG TO TRAINING WITH THEM IN MY BOY CLOTHES.

WE DON'T REALLY KNOW WHAT'S GOING TO HAPPEN. BUT ONE THING'S FOR SURE—WE'RE GOING TO FIGHT!

I KNOW I CAN'T BE A BACHA POSH FOREVER. BUT A LITTLE PART OF ME WILL ALWAYS BE MAHYAR.

LIVING A MAN'S LIFE TO BE FREE

Anyone have a problem with my way of life?

CALAMITY JANE

For hundreds of years, women have been changing their appearance to enjoy the same rights and freedoms as men. Take Agnodice, for example, the first female midwife in ancient Greece, and the famous Calamity Jane, the sharpshooter on horseback who wore men's clothing. They fought for women's liberation and dressed like men because they didn't want to be limited to being wives and mothers. The tradition of bacha posh in Afghanistan is said to date back as far as the year 900, to the court of the country's rulers. It's difficult to say how extensive the practice has been since then, but it is thought to have grown when the Taliban banned women from going out in public without a man. Mothers have raised their daughters as bacha posh to give them more freedom.

But when they reach adolescence and must switch to living as a girl, it can be very challenging for them to fit into society. They became another gender, not because they identified as male, but for freedom and safety. The change back to being a girl can be brutal and traumatic and may also lead to questions about gender identity.

In countries all around the world, most babies are labeled at birth as a boy or a girl according to their anatomy. This determines the way they grow up and their role in society. But some people's gender identity differs from the label they are given. The term *transgender* is used to refer to a person who identifies with a different gender. The word *gender* refers to a person's identity, and the word *sex* is based solely on the anatomy of a person's body.

WHAT, I'M NOT ALLOWED TO BECAUSE I'M A WOMAN? HA! LET'S SEE ABOUT THAT!

WHAT IS A PATRIARCHAL SOCIETY?

The word *patriarchy* dates to ancient times and has its roots in the Greek language. Historically it referred to a father's authority over his wife and children as head of the family.

A patriarchal society, therefore, is a society in which men wield all the power. It's a society that oppresses and excludes women. It's a society that dictates the daily lives of women. It's a society in which men make all the decisions and are the only ones allowed to work, vote and even have a say in everyday choices, as if women don't matter. Inequalities like these are often not clearly acknowledged, and women find themselves discriminated against from one generation to the next.

Isn't it kind of annoying how much of a male bias there is in the English language? You know, when people automatically say things like "Hey, guys," even if there's only one boy in a group of girls? The male form tends to be dominant in many languages because most cultures around the world have traditionally been patriarchal to some extent. Times are changing, but old habits can be hard to break. And in some places, it's even illegal to try to change things. Too many women are still deprived of freedom and rights over their own bodies, as well as the right to study, work and express their opinions. And the list goes on!

WOMEN IN AFGHANISTAN

Let's take a quick look at the history of women's rights in Afghanistan. Women gained the right to vote in 1919. In the 1960s and 1970s, many women were able to work and study, but women's rights were still fragile. Then the country entered an era of armed conflicts. Women were among the first victims. Rights were stripped away, and violence against women increased.

In 1996 a group of armed men called the Taliban set out to force their vision of the world on as many people and places as possible, in Afghanistan and Pakistan. The Taliban took power and imposed some very strict rules based on the way they interpret the religion of Islam. They applied Sharia law.

When that government was overturned in favor of an Islamic republic, women in cities were able to make some progress. With international aid, girls

Women bear the brunt of the merciless Taliban regime. Women are forced to wear burkas with full veils that cover their faces completely. They're victims of violence, and they aren't allowed to go to school, vote, work or go out in public without male company. Even their sons have more freedom than they do.

returned to school in the capital, Kabul. Some were able to go to university and to work—even in high-powered jobs and government positions. But in 2021 the country fell back into the hands of the Taliban. They reinstated Sharia law and took away all the new rights and freedoms.

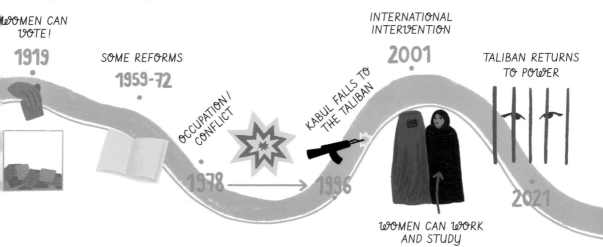

WOMEN CAN VOTE!

1919

SOME REFORMS

1959-72

OCCUPATION/ CONFLICT

1978

KABUL FALLS TO THE TALIBAN

1996

INTERNATIONAL INTERVENTION

2001

TALIBAN RETURNS TO POWER

2021

WOMEN CAN WORK AND STUDY

EDUCATED GIRLS ARE DANGEROUS

In Afghanistan, up to 70 percent of women don't know how to read or write. Access to education is an issue, as poverty forces more than a million children to work. But the Taliban forbids teenage girls from going to school, and thousands of schools have no dedicated building.

It's obvious that educating girls is good for society. When women are given responsibilities, they become agents of change and can shape their own futures. Educated girls have power. For the strictest of governments, that's terrifying. Educated women don't live in the shadow of the men in their families—they are seen as people. In 2017 activist Laleh Osmany and many more Afghan women founded the #WhereIsMyName campaign on social media. Together they took a stand. They refused to be defined by their male relatives and campaigned for their names to be visible.

In 2012 Malala Yousafzai, a young woman in Pakistan, was shot by the Taliban while riding a school bus. Her ordeal only strengthened her resolve to change the world. She was awarded the Nobel Peace Prize and now devotes her life to the fight for equal rights.

REST IN PEACE
MOTHER OF...
WIFE OF...

WHERE'S
MY NAME?

BEATING THE BANS

In Afghan society, it's considered indecent for girls to play sports. But a project called Skateistan has found an ingenious way around the ban on sports by introducing girls to skateboarding. It isn't a traditional sport, so it isn't outlawed. It's a daring initiative that has helped empower lots of girls.

In Iran some women defy the ban on cycling even if it means they might be arrested. Women there are also realizing that their phones are tools of freedom. Hijabs (headscarves) are mandatory, but Masih Alinejad started a movement on social media that encouraged women to hold up their scarves and take selfies with their hair flying free. In 2022 the morality police arrested Mahsa Amini for violating Islamic law by not wearing her veil properly. She died a few days later. Her death led to a huge wave of protests in Iran, first by women, then by men too.

For a long time women in Iran were banned from attending soccer games, despite there being no actual law preventing them from going. Eager to cheer on their team, some Iranian women wore fake beards, mustaches and wigs to sneak past security guards. One of them, Sahar Khodayari, was arrested by the authorities in 2019, and her tragic death was front-page news in countries around the world. Iran now allows thousands of women to attend soccer matches, provided they are seated separately from men and remain under police protection.

Some secret and not-so-secret sports clubs do exist for women to get together and gain confidence, share a passion for sports and even learn how to defend themselves.

DR. HABIBA SARĀBI

The first Afghan woman and activist to become a governor in the country and one of only four women to negotiate peace with the Taliban (2002)

KHALIDA POPAL

Founder of the first Afghan women's soccer team (2007) who went on to launch and direct the Girl Power organization (2014)

MARYAM DURANI

Militant and activist who single-handedly started and managed Merman Radio, promoting women's rights (2009)

NILOOFAR RAHMANI

First female pilot in the Afghan Air Force (2012)

HOSNA JALIL

First woman to be appointed to a high position in Afghanistan's Ministry of Interior Affairs (2018)

MASOMAH ALI ZADA

First female Afghan cyclist to compete in the Olympic Games (2020)

Plus, there's Soosan Firooz, Afghanistan's first female rapper; Fawzia Koofi, first female deputy speaker of the Afghan parliament; Negin Khpalwak, first Afghan female orchestra conductor; Manizha Talash, Afghanistan's first female break-dancer; Suhaila Siddiq, who was a surgeon and the first female general in Afghanistan; and many more inspiring women.

THE FUTURE IS FEMALE

Before the Taliban's latest rule in Afghanistan, women were playing a more active role in the country. Thousands of girls went to school and university and were empowered to work in professions essential for peace and stability. The courage of Afghan women enabled them to become lawyers, doctors, police officers, journalists, judges, teachers, engineers, athletes and even politicians. Many have been pioneers in their field, leading by example and paving the way for thousands of girls to follow in their footsteps.

Today Afghan society has changed. Women have protested against the Taliban in Kabul, despite the danger and threats of gunfire. Others continue to practice their profession in secret or have posted photos of their colorful traditional clothing on social media. These are ways to remind themselves that their culture is not the same as what's dictated by the Taliban. The future is uncertain for Afghan women, and it's hard for them to have hope. Many who are living in exile want to return as soon as they can to change their country or do what they can to help from overseas. Others who had no choice but to remain in the country continue to risk their lives to fight for their fundamental rights.

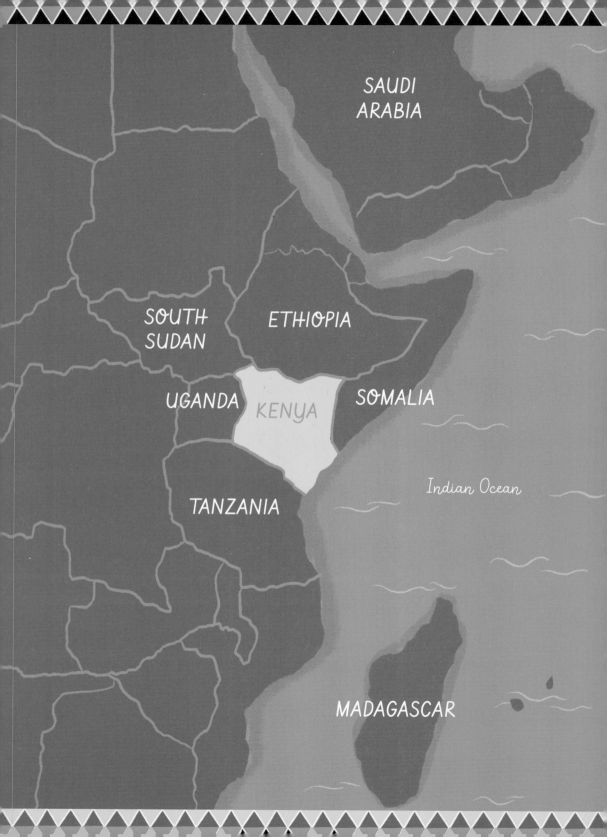

MAKENA
KENYA

JAMBO.
My name is Makena.

MAKENA

IN SWAHILI, MAKENA MEANS "BRINGER OF HAPPINESS."

I live in the
SAMBURU DISTRICT.

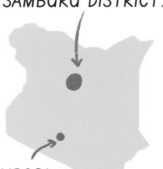

NAIROBI,
the capital city

I LIVE WITH MY COMMUNITY IN THE SAVANNA, CLOSE TO A NATURE RESERVE.

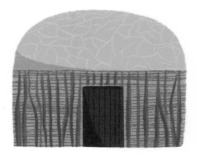

When I wake up, I admire the beautiful scenery

and hope I'll see some wildlife.

I SPEND A LOT OF TIME WITH THE WOMEN IN THE VILLAGE. TOGETHER WE FETCH WATER FOR OUR FAMILIES. IT'S A LONG WALK UNDER THE BLAZING SUN! IT RARELY RAINS HERE, AND EVERY YEAR THE DROUGHT GETS WORSE.

IT TAKES SEVERAL HOURS TO WALK TO THE RIVER AND BACK.

THAT MEANS I CAN'T GO TO SCHOOL. IT'S TOO FAR AWAY.

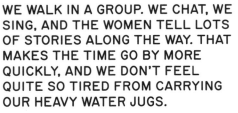

WE WALK IN A GROUP. WE CHAT, WE SING, AND THE WOMEN TELL LOTS OF STORIES ALONG THE WAY. THAT MAKES THE TIME GO BY MORE QUICKLY, AND WE DON'T FEEL QUITE SO TIRED FROM CARRYING OUR HEAVY WATER JUGS.

DURING THE DAY, MY FATHER HERDS GOATS.
WHEN HE RESTS, HE RESTS WITH THE OTHER
HERDSMEN. I DON'T SEE HIM VERY MUCH. THE
MEN KEEP TO THEMSELVES AND MAKE ALL THE
DECISIONS. THE WOMEN DON'T SPEAK UP.

NO ONE WOULD LISTEN TO THEM ANYWAY.

THERE'S A TRADITION HERE CALLED CUTTING. IT'S VERY DANGEROUS FOR GIRLS AND THEIR BODIES.

WHEN WE REACH PUBERTY, OUR MOTHER OR A FEMALE RELATIVE TAKES US TO SEE A WOMAN CALLED A *CUTTER*, WITHOUT TELLING US WHAT'S GOING TO HAPPEN. THAT WOMAN CUTS OFF PART OF OUR GENITALS. IT'S TYPICALLY THE LABIA OR THE CLITORIS.

WE HAVE NO CHOICE IN THE MATTER. GIRLS WHO RESIST ARE RESTRAINED.

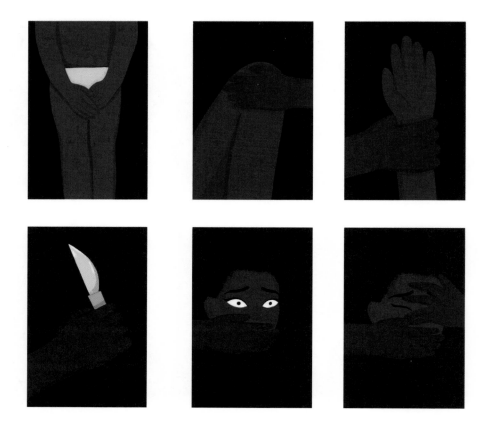

People say that without this, girls won't become women and they'll never find husbands.

MY FRIEND AÏSHA WAS FORCED TO MARRY AN OLDER MAN. THE CUTTER CAME TO HER HOME ON THE MORNING OF THE WEDDING. AÏSHA WAS TAKEN COMPLETELY BY SURPRISE. PEOPLE AROUND THE VILLAGE COULD HEAR HER SCREAMING IN PAIN.

AÏSHA HAS NEVER BEEN THE SAME SINCE.

MY MOTHER HAS TOLD ME IT WILL SOON BE MY TURN TO HAVE A PART OF ME CUT AWAY.

THAT WAY I'LL BE READY TO MARRY A MAN MY PARENTS CHOOSE FOR ME. IT DOESN'T MATTER IF HE'S TWICE MY AGE OR EVEN THREE OR FOUR TIMES OLDER THAN ME. THE MOST IMPORTANT THING IS FOR ME TO BE A WIFE.

LIKE A GOOD GIRL, I AGREED. BUT I WAS TERRIFIED!
I TOLD AÏSHA ABOUT IT RIGHT AWAY.

THIS SHOULD NEVER HAPPEN AGAIN.

I KEEP THINKING ABOUT WHAT'S
COMING FOR ME AND FOR MY LITTLE
SISTER AS WELL, BECAUSE ONE DAY
IT WILL BE HER TURN.

IS THERE ANY WAY OUT OF IT?

LATER, WHEN WE WENT TO FETCH WATER, AN ELDER TOLD ME ABOUT TUMAI, A VILLAGE FAR AWAY WHERE WOMEN ALL LIVE TOGETHER, WITHOUT ANY MEN!

No marriage or cutting here!

SHE TOLD ME THAT WHEN SHE BECAME A MOTHER, SHE REFUSED TO TAKE HER DAUGHTER TO THE CUTTER. ALL HER FAMILY AND FRIENDS TURNED AGAINST HER AND THREATENED TO BANISH HER FROM THE VILLAGE. IN THE END, SHE HAD NO CHOICE BUT TO AGREE TO THE CUTTING.

TUMAI

SHE KNOWS THAT BY HELPING US, SHE CAN SAVE OTHER GIRLS FROM BEING CUT.

SHE TOLD ME HOW TO GET TO TUMAI. HER ADVICE GAVE ME CONFIDENCE.

THERE'S NO TIME TO LOSE. I KNOW MY PARENTS ARE GOING TO MARRY ME OFF SOON!

AÏSHA AND I AGREED TO MEET IN A SECRET PLACE
BEFORE SUNRISE, WITH MY LITTLE SISTER.

WE WERE STILL HALF-ASLEEP WHEN WE LEFT THE VILLAGE.
I WALKED AWAY WITHOUT LOOKING BACK. I HAVE TO STAY
STRONG FOR MY SISTER. SHE DOESN'T REALLY UNDERSTAND
WHAT'S HAPPENING. WE RAN THROUGH THE BUSH AT FIRST
BEFORE WALKING FOR TWO DAYS. WE'VE HAD TO DO MOST OF
THE WALKING AT NIGHT. IT'S HOT IN THE DAYTIME, AND WE
DON'T WANT TO CROSS PATHS WITH ANYONE.

IN THE DISTANCE WE CAN SEE ELEPHANTS LOOKING FOR
WATER. MY PEOPLE DON'T LIKE ELEPHANTS BECAUSE
THEY EAT THE GRASS THE CATTLE NEED. BUT I'VE ALWAYS
ADMIRED THEM. WE'RE READY FOR ANYTHING, BUT WE
WON'T GO BACK TO THE VILLAGE.

NOW I CAN SEE MANYATTA HUTS
IN THE DISTANCE. THEY'RE
COVERED IN ACACIA BRANCHES.

WE'VE MADE IT TO TUMAI AT LAST!

THE WOMEN AND CHILDREN GIVE US A
WARM WELCOME WHEN WE GET THERE.
WE TELL THEM OUR STORY. MANY
OF THEM HAVE ESCAPED FROM THE
CUTTER AND FROM FORCED MARRIAGE.

ALL OF THEM HAVE RUN AWAY FROM MEN AND THEIR VIOLENCE. LIKE SISTERS, EVERYONE HERE HELPS EACH OTHER. WE FEEL SAFE RIGHT AWAY.

WE'VE ARRIVED ON A SPECIAL DAY. IT'S A DAY OF CELEBRATION.

WE APPLY A GREASY PASTE OF RED DIRT TO OUR
FACES, AND THEN THE CEREMONY CAN BEGIN.

WE ALL SING TOGETHER. EVERY MONTH THE WOMEN
CELEBRATE THE SPIRITS OF NATURE SO THEY WILL
BRING RAIN AND PROTECT THE VILLAGE.

"May the rain bring us joy and abundance.
May Mother Nature bring us all her riches."

WE POUR GOAT'S MILK INTO THE SACRED RIVER AND START A FIRE. WE DANCE AND CLAP OUR HANDS TO THE SOUND OF OUR NECKLACES CLINKING TOGETHER. WE FEEL SO CONNECTED!

THE MEN IN THE SURROUNDING
VILLAGES HAVE A NICKNAME FOR
THE WOMEN OF TUMAI:

"LIONESSES OF THE BUSH"

NOW, EVERY MORNING, I TELL
MYSELF I'M LUCKY TO LIVE
HERE. FOR THE FIRST TIME IN
MY LIFE, I CAN GO TO SCHOOL.

I'M LEARNING ENGLISH. I'M
LEARNING TO READ AND WRITE.

THE TEACHER TALKS TO
US ABOUT OUR RIGHTS AND
OUR BODIES.

I REALLY GET THE IMPRESSION THAT MY TRUE LIFE IS BEGINNING NOW. BUT WHEN I THINK ABOUT THE FRIENDS AND COUSINS I LEFT BEHIND IN THE VILLAGE, AND WHEN I THINK ABOUT MY MOTHER...

...I FEEL SO SAD.

I WOULD LOVE TO GO BACK AND EXPLAIN TO THEM THAT GIRLS CAN SAY NO.

AND THAT THE TRADITIONS THAT CAUSE US HARM AND PREVENT US FROM LIVING FREELY MUST STOP.

ONE DAY AT SCHOOL, SOME PEOPLE FROM THE RETETI ELEPHANT SANCTUARY COME TO TALK TO US ABOUT THEIR WORK.

THE MANAGER OF THE SANCTUARY IS A WOMAN. I DIDN'T THINK THAT WAS EVEN POSSIBLE!

THEY SAVE ORPHANED ELEPHANTS WHOSE MOTHERS WERE KILLED BY POACHERS. THEN THEY HELP THE YOUNG ELEPHANTS JOIN A NEW HERD.

VILLAGES FOR WOMEN

In the Samburu region of Kenya, the nomadic communities of herdsmen are patriarchal. Women can only be wives, have children and raise them. Plus, they work all day without having a say in any family decisions, and they own no property. Their voices are never heard.

One day a group of women found the courage to break the silence and speak out against violence. Many of them were survivors of sexual assault by British soldiers. Instead of supporting them, the women's husbands accused them of dishonoring them. They rejected them. Powerless, the women turned to their government for help but were ignored. In 1990, 15 of these women went looking for some land to build a new life on. They built their own sanctuary and

Rebecca Lolosoli is one of the women who founded Umoja. For 30 years, she has been raising awareness around the world about the violence suffered by women in Samburu and across Africa.

founded the village of Umoja, which means "unity" in Swahili.

Umoja welcomes women who are fleeing from violence, female genital mutilation (cutting) and forced marriage. They welcome widowed women too. Men who feel threatened and can't handle the thought of women being independent have tried to shut the village down. And failed! These women are pioneers who decided to resist, rather than going back to their husbands. For protection, they hired two Samburu warriors to stand guard over Umoja day and night. The community has set an example for women to build more small matriarchal societies in Kenya. Now there are Tumai, Nang'ida, Mokupori and others.

THE LAST MATRIARCHAL SOCIETIES

There are a few matriarchal societies in the world where women make the decisions for their community. Property (homes, land and belongings) is passed down from mothers to their daughters, and so are family names. Girls are the connection between generations. These societies look up to Mother Nature, and through her they celebrate the cycle of life. To give birth to a girl is an honor. That's a rare custom in this world! Matriarchal societies never seek to dominate or perpetuate violence against men.

It's usual for several generations to live under the same roof, and everyone helps one another. That's the case in the Mosuo tribal community in China. There, the dabu—the eldest woman—is the head of the household. Their community is courageous in resisting the country's policy of valuing sons over daughters.

Despite their importance, women in matriarchal societies rarely hold political and economic powers. When property and traditions are passed down from mother to daughter, it's called a matrilineal rather than a matriarchal society. In the matrilineal

The Minangkabau in Indonesia is the world's largest matrilineal society, with six million people. We have a lot to learn from them and from other matrilineal societies like the Khasi people of India and the Akans of Ghana!

community of Juchitán, Mexico, women are the heart of the economy, but even so, violence against women is a serious problem. Sixty percent of the women who live there are victims of domestic violence.

LET'S TALK ABOUT CUTTING

The practice of cutting, or female genital mutilation (FGM), is banned in almost all countries around the world. Yet even today, six girls are subjected to FGM every minute. The practice continues on every continent on the planet.

It's not an easy subject to talk about. It's a brutal act that involves cutting off some of the vulva (the outer parts of the female genitals), including the labia and/ or the clitoris, which is associated with sexual pleasure. Families that insist on FGM think they are passing on a tradition. But the truth is, cutting a woman's genitals and preventing pleasure is a way of controlling her body and her sexuality. Victims of this practice often suffer severe physical and mental side effects for the rest of their lives. It's such a taboo subject that even women who have been subjected to FGM repeat the practice with their own daughters because they fear being rejected.

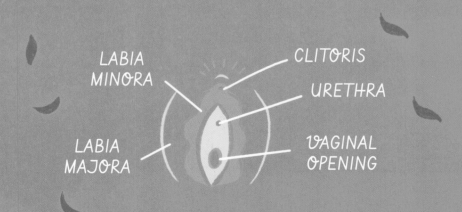

LABIA MINORA

CLITORIS

URETHRA

LABIA MAJORA

VAGINAL OPENING

ENEMY NUMBER ONE: THE CLITORIS

In the fourth century, Christianity associated the body's sex organs with the sin of Adam and Eve. As the story went, it was all Eve's fault for biting the apple! Women were made out to be sinners, and the clitoris was seen as the mark of the devil. What the heck! In the 1600s attitudes changed, and people came to think that pleasure was a necessary part of getting pregnant.

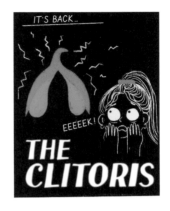

Then, in the 1800s, things took a different turn. In Europe at this time, FGM was used to treat women for hysteria and migraines and even as a "cure" for masturbation and homosexuality! It didn't help when the psychoanalyst Sigmund Freud came along with some very unscientific theories about the clitoris and the vagina. It seemed like there were plenty of reasons back then to control women and their bodies. Between 1900 and 1950, it was almost like the clitoris had just disappeared. It was only in 1998 that a doctor named Helen O'Connell revealed that the clitoris is more than just a little button on the outside of the vulva. The clitoris extends into the body, and the whole thing can be up to 4.5 inches (12 centimeters) long and as wide as 2.5 inches (7 centimeters)!

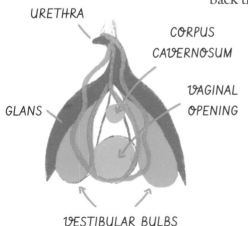

URETHRA

CORPUS CAVERNOSUM

VAGINAL OPENING

GLANS

VESTIBULAR BULBS

There are many myths about the clitoris. It's sometimes described as an "unnecessary" male element of female anatomy. The Bambara people in Mali think the clitoris is like a bee's sting that could hurt or kill a woman's husband. And the Maasai of East Africa are said to believe that women who are not cut will be haunted by the spirits of their ancestors.

FORCED INTO MARRIAGE

Forced marriages are arranged between families and organized without the girl's agreement. The wife's family gives property or money to the husband's family. This is called a *dowry*. The thing is, it's not exactly a gift. Plus, the younger the girl is, the lower the price of the dowry, so it's cheaper for poor families to marry their daughters off early. Twelve million girls are married before the age of 18 each year. Many of these are in India, the country with the highest rate of child marriages in the world. Girls are seen as property to be sold and exchanged.

But why not give girls a choice in the matter? Often it's because the poorest families can't afford to pay for their daughters' education or they choose to invest in their sons' education instead. They might save money, but once their daughters are married, they'll never go back to school. They'll depend on their husbands for life. They'll have no choice in their future, and chances are their own daughters won't have an education either.

HOW TO FIGHT FORCED MARRIAGE:

EDUCATION

ECONOMIC FREEDOM

MALE ALLIES

A NEW LIFE

On Kenya's Samburu National Reserve, access to education for girls is limited. They don't have time to go to school because they're so busy fetching water for their communities to go about daily life. At the same time, the elephants on the reserve are also threatened by extinction. The Reteti Elephant Sanctuary was created to save orphaned elephants whose herds have left them behind.

In the elephant world, the eldest female rules the family. That's right—elephant herds are matriarchal societies too!

Some Samburu women got involved in the project and became elephant keepers. They started a revolution! Sasha Dorothy Lowuekuduk was one of the first women to work at the sanctuary and have men report to her. She's setting an example for Samburu children, especially girls!

In Zimbabwe women are active in the fight against poaching. As park rangers they protect wildlife and patrol to stop poachers. Many of them have escaped from violent homes, FGM and forced marriages and are now starting a new life. They're fighters. They're brave, and they're respected. Poaching has declined by 80 percent since the female rangers started their squad and set about building sustainable relationships with communities.

THE RITUALS OF BECOMING A WOMAN

Growing up and becoming an adult is something that deserves to be celebrated! There are 42 tribes in Kenya, and each has its own coming-of-age ritual. Some associations, and even some women who used to be cutters themselves, have advocated for alternative rituals and a ban on FGM.

In Kenya some Maasai girls give their elders a blanket. By accepting this gift, the elders agree that they will no longer tolerate FGM and forced marriage. And as future husbands, warriors who stand up against the practice of FGM will bring about a change in society. Villages embracing new traditions have seen positive changes in their communities.

These rites of passage are an opportunity to sing, to celebrate and to honor every girl. In North America, girls in Apache Nations are honored with a Sunrise Ceremony that involves carrying out specific rituals and passing tests to prove they are ready to become adults. They learn how to do many things, sleep in tepees, dance every evening and are given their new Apache names. Girls are proud to take part. They feel valued and they feel strong.

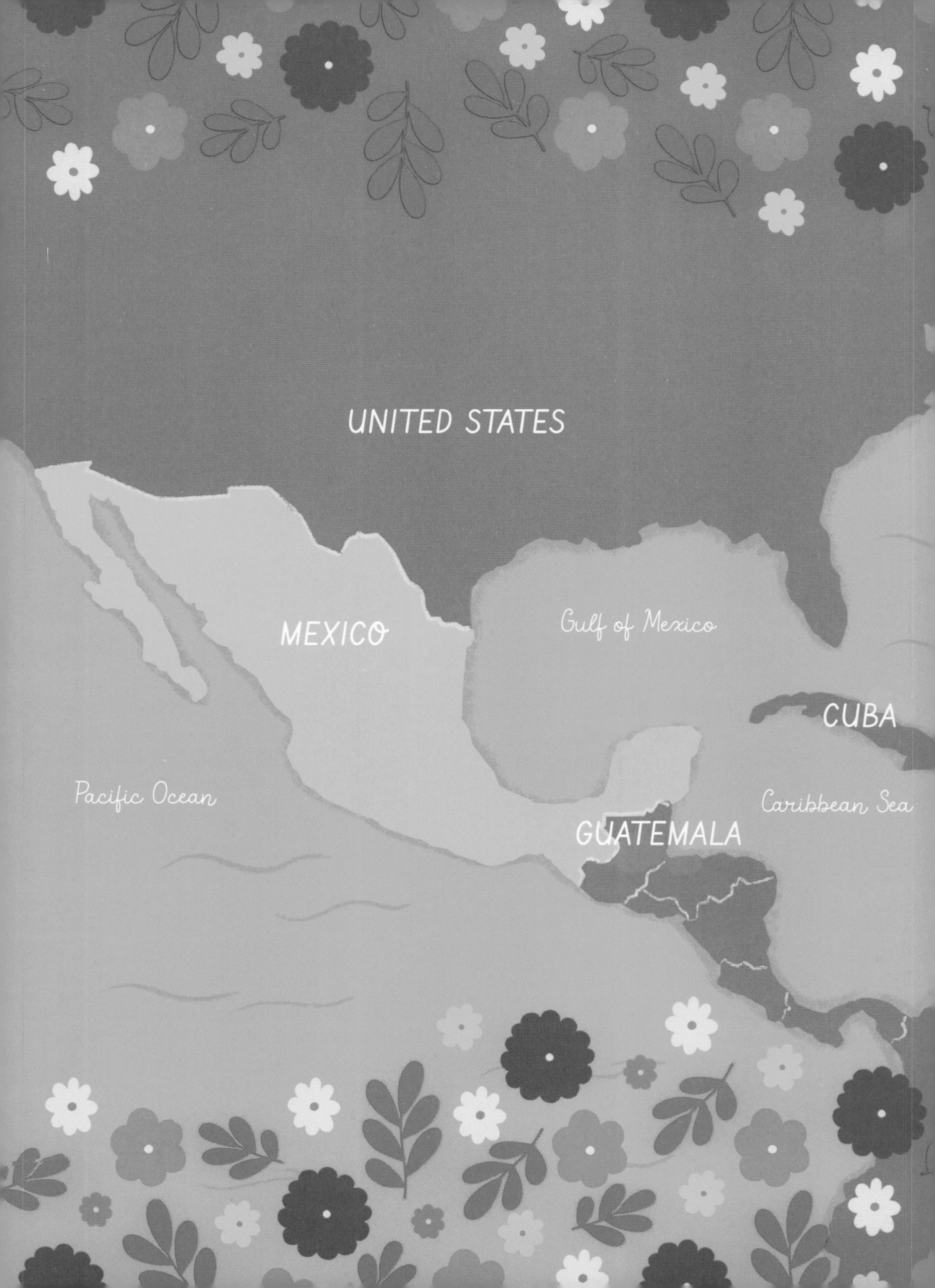
UNITED STATES
MEXICO
Gulf of Mexico
CUBA
Pacific Ocean
Caribbean Sea
GUATEMALA

LUISA

MEXICO

NI UNA MÁS

¡HOLA!
My name is Luisa.

LUiSA

MY NAME MEANS "GLORIOUS WARRIOR."

I LIVE WITH MY PARENTS, MY BIG SISTER AND MY BROTHER IN A NEIGHBORHOOD WHERE THE HOUSES ARE BUILT CLOSE TOGETHER AND STACKED ON TOP OF EACH OTHER.

I live in the STATE OF MEXICO, near MEXICO CITY, the capital.

From my window I can see the rooftops and the brightly colored houses of the whole city.

MY GRANDMOTHER LIVES RIGHT ACROSS THE STREET. SHE LIKES TO MAKE DELICIOUS FOOD FOR OUR FAMILY AND OFTEN INVITES US OVER FOR DINNER.

WE ALL GO TO CHURCH TOGETHER EVERY WEEK. SHE AND I ARE VERY CLOSE. IT'S GOOD THAT SHE LIVES NEARBY. WHEN THERE ARE ARGUMENTS AT HOME, I GO TO HER PLACE TO ESCAPE.

THE WOMEN IN THE NEIGHBORHOOD ARE ALL FRIENDS. THEY HELP EACH OTHER OUT, LEND THINGS TO EACH OTHER AND CHAT FOR HOURS ON END. MANY OF THEM DON'T WORK BESIDES LOOKING AFTER THEIR HOMES AND THEIR CHILDREN. MY MOTHER WORKS AS A CLEANER. MY FATHER HAS A JOB TOO. HE WORKS ON CONSTRUCTION SITES.

I LOVE MY FAMILY, AND I LIKE MY CITY AND ALL ITS COLORS. IT'S FULL OF PRETTY STAIRWAYS AND ALLEYS.

BUT I DON'T FEEL SAFE IN MY NEIGHBORHOOD. THERE ARE OFTEN FIGHTS, AND PEOPLE HURT EACH OTHER. I THINK IT USUALLY HAS SOMETHING TO DO WITH DRUGS. SO I JUST TRY TO BE CAREFUL.

ONE TIME, THERE WERE A LOT OF PEOPLE ON THE BUS AND I FELT A HAND TOUCHING MY THIGH. USUALLY WHEN SOMETHING BOTHERS ME, I REACT IMMEDIATELY. BUT IN THAT MOMENT, I WAS TERRIFIED.

LUCKILY, I SOON CAME TO MY SENSES AND GOT OFF THE BUS AT THE NEXT STOP.

NONE OF THE PEOPLE AROUND ME REACTED AT ALL, EVEN THOSE WHO SAW WHAT WAS HAPPENING. I RAN STRAIGHT HOME WITHOUT STOPPING!

WHEN I GOT THERE, MY FATHER SAID, "WHAT KIND OF OUTFIT IS THAT? YOU'RE ASKING FOR TROUBLE, LUISA." AND MY MOTHER ADDED, "MAYBE YOU LOOKED AT THAT MAN A CERTAIN WAY OR DID SOMETHING TO LEAD HIM ON."

I KNOW I DIDN'T DO ANYTHING WRONG. HE'S THE ONE AT FAULT, NOT ME! NOW I AVOID TAKING THE BUS. THAT DOESN'T STOP MEN IN THE STREET FROM HARASSING ME, THOUGH. I WEAR HEADPHONES TO MAKE IT LOOK LIKE I CAN'T HEAR THEM, AND I WALK QUICKLY. I HAVE TO STAY ALERT!

If I wear shorts when the weather is hot, I know men are going to make comments again. I avoid certain streets.

I try to walk with a male friend.

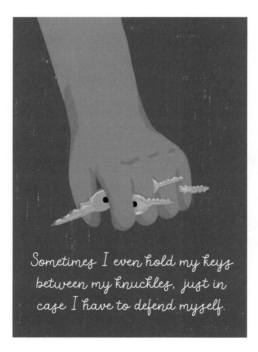

Sometimes I even hold my keys between my knuckles, just in case I have to defend myself.

If I sense that someone's following me, I pretend to make a phone call while staying alert.

FAVORITES
☆ Mom
☆ María
☆ Dad

THINGS ARE NO BETTER AT SCHOOL. THE BOYS
HARASS THE GIRLS. I'M PRETTY SURE THAT ALL
OF MY FRIENDS HAVE HAD THEIR SKIRTS LIFTED
UP OR HAVE HAD TO DEAL WITH COMMENTS
ABOUT THEIR BODIES. THE TEACHERS JUST
IGNORE IT.

HEY, WHAT IS WRONG WITH YOU?!

THIS IS LEO, A BOY IN MY CLASS. I KNOW HE
LIKES ME. HE SAID SO TO ONE OF MY FRIENDS.
BUT EVERY TIME HE COMES NEAR ME, HE
GETS ALL WEIRD. HE AND HIS FRIENDS HAVE
PUSHED ME AROUND AND TRIPPED ME.

I ALWAYS TELL MYSELF IT'S
NO BIG DEAL—THEY'RE JUST
TEASING. BUT I DON'T LIKE IT.

LEO SHOVED ME TO THE GROUND, AND IT HURT. HE AND HIS FRIENDS LAUGHED. AND THEN HE HELPED ME UP AGAIN. FURIOUS, I YELLED AT HIM AND SHOVED HIM AS HARD AS I COULD AGAINST THE WALL. ALL HIS FRIENDS LAUGHED AT HIM.

"HA, HA! THE SHAME! PUSHED AROUND BY A GIRL!"

RIGHT AT THAT MOMENT, A TEACHER CAME BY. HE WOULDN'T LISTEN TO ME. HE TOLD ME TO STOP DRAWING ATTENTION TO MYSELF. HE SAID I SOUNDED CRAZY, YELLING LIKE THAT.

IF LEO LIKES ME, WHY DOES HE ONLY SHOW IT BY GOOFING OFF? SOME OF MY FRIENDS SAY I'M EXAGGERATING. THEY SAY I'M LUCKY HE'S INTERESTED IN ME.

TODAY IS MY SISTER MARÍA'S QUINCE AÑOS PARTY. WE'VE BEEN WAITING FOR THIS MOMENT FOR MONTHS. MY PARENTS SAVED UP A LOT OF MONEY TO CELEBRATE HER 15TH BIRTHDAY AND COMING OF AGE WITH A GATHERING OF FAMILY AND FRIENDS.

MY GRANDMOTHER IS STYLING MY SISTER'S HAIR IN THE BATHROOM BEFORE WE GO TO MASS.

THEY BOUGHT HER THE DRESS OF HER DREAMS. THERE'LL BE LOTS TO EAT AND DRINK.

WHEN MY SISTER REACHES HER ARMS OUT TO ME, I NOTICE SOME MARKS ON HER WRISTS.

I GLANCE AT MY GRANDMOTHER, AND SHE LOOKS HORRIFIED. "WHAT ARE THOSE BRUISES, MARÍA? WHO DID THIS TO YOU?"

QUICKLY MY SISTER SLIPS SOME BRACELETS ON HER WRISTS TO HIDE THE MARKS.

MY GRANDMOTHER CAN'T STAND VIOLENCE. SHE TAKES A CLOSER LOOK AT MY SISTER AND FINDS SHE HAS BRUISES ON HER THIGHS TOO. IT'S OBVIOUS THAT SOMEONE HAS HURT HER.

"WAS IT JUAN? IS HE THE ONE WHO DID THIS?"

I'VE HEARD MARÍA AND HER BOYFRIEND ARGUING BEFORE, AND YELLING IN THE STREET, BUT I NEVER THOUGHT IT WOULD COME TO THIS.

MY SISTER RUSHES OUT OF THE BATHROOM WITHOUT SAYING A WORD. I KNOW MY GRANDMOTHER DOESN'T WANT TO RUIN MARÍA'S DAY, BUT I DON'T THINK SHE'LL LET THIS DROP.

WEEKS GO BY, AND I HAVEN'T SAID ANYTHING TO MY SISTER ABOUT WHAT HAPPENED. SHE'S QUITE SHY, AND I DON'T WANT TO UPSET HER.

WHEN I GET UP THIS MORNING, I FIND MY MOTHER IN THE KITCHEN. SHE LOOKS EXHAUSTED. MARÍA DIDN'T COME HOME LAST NIGHT. THAT'S NOT LIKE HER AT ALL.

MY MOTHER CALLED THE POLICE, BUT THEY DIDN'T TAKE HER SERIOUSLY. MARÍA'S FRIENDS AND HER BOYFRIEND DON'T KNOW ANYTHING. WE'RE ALL VERY WORRIED.

TWO DAYS GO BY WITHOUT ANY NEWS. THERE'S STILL NO SIGN OF MARÍA AT SCHOOL EITHER. MY MOTHER HAS GONE TO THE POLICE STATION SEVERAL TIMES, BUT NO ONE THERE THINKS THE SITUATION IS URGENT.

"YOU'RE WORRYING ABOUT NOTHING. YOU KNOW WHAT THEY'RE LIKE AT THAT AGE."

I DON'T JUST WANT TO SIT HERE AND DO NOTHING. SO I GO TO SEE MARÍA'S BOYFRIEND, BUT HE GETS MAD AT ME.

THIS IS A NIGHTMARE. ANYTHING MIGHT HAVE HAPPENED. I IMAGINE THE WORST KINDS OF SCENARIOS.

WE GO KNOCKING ON OUR NEIGHBORS' DOORS TO TELL THEM MARÍA IS MISSING. MAYBE THEY CAN HELP US.

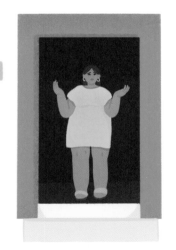

216

ONE NEIGHBOR LOST HER OWN DAUGHTER A FEW YEARS AGO. THE POLICE HAVE NEVER SOLVED THE CASE. EVERYTHING SUGGESTS HER EX-BOYFRIEND WAS INVOLVED.

CUTS AND BRUISES

THREATS

AND LIFE GOES ON FOR HIM AS IF NOTHING HAPPENED

SINCE THEN OUR NEIGHBOR HAS BECOME A MEMBER OF AN ASSOCIATION FOR THE FAMILIES OF VICTIMS OF VIOLENCE. SHE INVITES US TO ONE OF THEIR MEETINGS AND REASSURES US THAT WE'LL BE HELPED AND SUPPORTED.

You are not alone.

WE MEET WOMEN OF ALL AGES. THERE ARE SISTERS, FRIENDS, MOTHERS AND GRANDMOTHERS. THEY HAVE ALL LOST SOMEONE THEY LOVE. SOMEONE WHO'S MISSING—OR MURDERED.

JUSTICIA PARA MARÍA

JUSTICE FOR MARÍA

THERE ARE ALSO WOMEN WHO ARE SURVIVORS OF VIOLENCE AND WANT TO TAKE ACTION FOR JUSTICE. THEIR COURAGE GIVES US STRENGTH.

TONIGHT WE'LL PUT UP POSTERS AND SPRAY MESSAGES ON WALLS SO THAT EVERYONE KNOWS MY SISTER IS MISSING.

WE ARE SAD AND WE ARE HURTING,
BUT WE ARE DETERMINED. THE POLICE
SAY THEY HAVE NO EVIDENCE, SO THEY
WON'T INVESTIGATE. WE ARE FURIOUS.

WE TELL THEM ABOUT THE BRUISES ON
MARÍA'S BODY. THEY SAY IT'S NO BIG DEAL
AND TELL US WE SHOULD JUST LET IT
DROP. BUT IT'S A BIG DEAL FOR US.

LUCKILY, THE ASSOCIATION AND THE WOMEN IN THE NEIGHBORHOOD
ARE THERE TO SUPPORT US. MY FATHER IS VERY UPSET, BUT HE IS
ALSO VERY INVOLVED. HE SPENDS HIS TIME CALLING AND REACHING
OUT TO PEOPLE TO TRY TO FIND OUT WHAT HAPPENED. WE FEEL
COMPLETELY ABANDONED.

IF NONE OF THE AUTHORITIES
WILL LISTEN TO US, WE WILL
ALL GO OUT AND PROTEST.
TOGETHER WE WILL SPEAK OUT
FOR THE MISSING WOMEN AND
THE VICTIMS. WE WILL SPEAK
OUT TO END ALL THE VIOLENCE
AGAINST WOMEN.

WHAT IS FEMICIDE?

Femicide is the most extreme form of gender-based violence against women. Femicide is the killing of women and girls by men, often a partner or ex-partner, although sometimes the perpetrator is a friend, a family member or a stranger. Victims of femicide may be young or old and from any social background. Femicide is an important term. In the past, many acts of violence against women were called "crimes of passion." But these crimes are sexist and have nothing to do with love. In 2007 the crime of femicide was written into Mexico's Federal Penal Code. On average, at least 10 women are killed every day in Mexico. Latin America has the highest concentration of gender-based violence in the world.

Have you ever heard the term *witch hunt* and wondered where it originated? During the Renaissance period in Europe, the church accused some women of witchcraft. They were sentenced to death and often burned at the stake. But these women were not really witches. They were women who threatened men and their power—because of their knowledge, their age, their rejection of motherhood and their independence.

"A WOMAN WITH OPINIONS! SHE MUST BE STOPPED!"

"SO BEING A WOMAN IS STILL A PROBLEM NOW, JUST LIKE IT WAS BACK THEN?"

A WORLD WITHOUT WOMEN?

Sadly, femicide happens for many reasons. One is macho culture, which disrespects women and values the superiority of men. Another is political, and happens when decisions are made to limit women's rights to things like abortion. Gang and drug-related violence is another factor. In some countries, the police and the government do not necessarily take an unbiased approach to law enforcement. Sometimes police officers are bribed (given money) to not investigate a case. This is called *corruption*. In Mexico most femicides go unpunished.

In some cultures, boys are favored so heavily that parents may choose to end a pregnancy to avoid having a girl, or they may abandon their baby if it's a girl. This is often the case in China, for example.

On March 9, 2020, a group of Mexican women wanted to show what the world would look like without them. On the day after International Women's Day, some organizations called for women across the country to go on strike. For one day, thousands of women protested against femicide and the failure of authorities to act. That day they did not go to work or to school. They did not even go out in public! Their slogan for the day—"Un día sin nosotras" (A day without us)—demonstrated how the country would grind to a halt without women.

In Asia, it's estimated that more than 150 million girls have "disappeared" in the last 30 years alone because of the practice of choosing boys over girls. In India, concerns about dowries and marriage are the main reason for this tragic sex-selection process. But the government is trying to turn the tide by offering bursaries for girls to go to school.

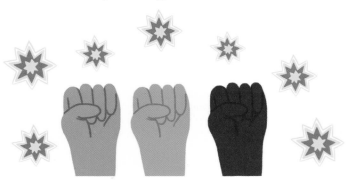

NORMALIZING VIOLENCE

From childhood, boys and girls are educated differently. It may not be intentional, but they often grow up in environments that define them based on gender and gender-based stereotypes. In some places in the world, boys are taught that they must be strong and not show their emotions. They are taught to use physical violence to solve conflict. By the same token, girls are expected to be well-behaved and keep their opinions to themselves. They don't get to make their own decisions. That way, they'll become perfect wives and mothers. This kind of education is suffocating girls. It's devaluing them and taking away their freedom. Boys are also having a hard time breaking free from the model they are expected to follow.

In some places in Mexico, the tradition of women being homemakers and men earning money for the household is reinforced by gang culture. Men must be macho and think nothing of violence. People think it's normal to belittle women. People think domestic violence is normal. And because it happens in the home, it's seen as a private matter and is not taken seriously. But it's clear that what is private is political. And things must change.

THE PROBLEM IS NOT WHAT I'M WEARING, IT'S THE WAY YOU'RE LOOKING AT ME.

THE STREETS ARE OURS

Public spaces can be dangerous places for girls, especially when they are alone. That doesn't mean they should have to stay at home, though. Unfortunately, many girls in Mexico and other countries have experienced some sort of harassment or physical violence on the street.

And often they get blamed for it. Somehow it's easier to ask them what they were doing outside on their own and question what they were wearing than it is to hold the offender accountable. But every person has the right to dress however they like. The real problem is the way other people look at them. In Mexico, the average age at which girls are exposed to harassment in public is seven. The Mexico City Metro is said to be one of the most dangerous public transit systems in the world for women. There have been reports of assaults and even attempted kidnappings. Taxis are not necessarily safe, and neither are the streets. To raise awareness about the problem, thousands of women have used the hashtag #MiPrimerAcoso (#MyFirstAssault) on social media to share their first experiences of harassment in public.

The government has now introduced women-only carriages on the metro. There are also some safe, private taxi services. Many women reluctantly choose to adapt and dress more conservatively so as not to draw attention to themselves. Solutions like these may have an immediate impact on women's safety, but they won't change anything in the long term. Most women don't report harassment. They know they'll likely be blamed and there won't be an investigation or punishment. Educating the authorities about gender issues will help them to help the victims.

A group of young women calling themselves Las Morras (The Girls) posted a video online of themselves walking through the streets of Mexico City. The video shows them being harassed by men with catcalls and comments about their appearance. The video has been viewed all over the world.

THE FEMINIST REVOLUTION

When the police don't take action and the government doesn't put the necessary measures in place, women have no option but to voice their anger in order to make things change. "¡Ya basta! (Enough is enough!)." The Ni Una Menos (Not One Less Woman) movement started in Argentina and spread throughout South America. Women mobilized, took to the streets and started a revolution that has fueled a new wave of feminist activism. They say they are the voice of the women

When investigations lead nowhere and justice is not served, many victims' families take it upon themselves to seek answers.

who are no longer here. These women are fighting for justice and calling for an end to gender-based violence and sexual harassment. They want to see measures implemented to protect victims and sound the alarm about the violence and harassment they suffer daily. The authorities have responded to these protests with violence. In 2020, police in Cancún even opened fire on the women who were protesting.

"MY FRIENDS PROTECT ME, BECAUSE THE POLICE DON'T!"

GIRLS WHO BREAK THE RULES

As crimes against women increase and violence goes unpunished, a sense of urgency is driving some young activists to take matters into their own hands. Words and demonstrations are no longer enough to express their anger, so they are taking radical action.

The feminist Bloque Negro (Black Bloc) movement in Mexico City aims to take back the streets for women and is fighting fear with fear. Young, masked women have marched bare-chested through the streets, vandalizing public property and starting fires in response to the violence they and their friends have experienced and the lack of support from authorities. They even occupied Mexico's Human Rights Commission building, making it their headquarters and a safe space for victims. They use social media to organize their events and raise awareness about the injustice. Their motto is "Never forgiven, never forgotten." And they will keep putting up posters and spraying graffiti on walls for as long as women remain victims.

The protesters must face sanctions for their actions. But society must also take action to prevent the violence by teaching boys about respect and consent.

SORORITY

The word *sorority* comes from the Latin noun *sororitas* ("sisterhood"), based on the Latin adjective *soror*, meaning "sister" or "cousin." It's the female equivalent of *fraternity*, or "brotherhood." There is something very empowering about the word. Sorority is about women being together and helping each other. Sorority has power. Women are campaigning for common issues, even though their experiences and struggles can be different. It's by supporting one another and joining forces that they will continue the feminist fight. Together women are driving the feminist revolution. Sorority is about women protecting each other and uniting against the patriarchy. Through rallies, gatherings and women's circles, we can all share our stories and give comfort and understanding to others— and remind ourselves that we are not alone.

"IF THEY TOUCH ONE OF US, THEY TOUCH US ALL. JUSTICE! JUSTICE!" *

* TRANSLATION OF LYRICS FROM "CANCIÓN SIN MIEDO" ("SONG WITHOUT FEAR") BY VIVIR QUINTANA. THIS SONG IS ABOUT THE VIOLENCE EXPERIENCED BY WOMEN AND HAS BECOME AN ANTHEM AT PROTESTS.

WHY BORN A GIRL?

When I was little, I was a bit of a daredevil. I used to scream and shout a lot. But at the same time, I liked to play with Barbies, collect comics, read and do "girly" stuff. I never really thought about things. I just went with the flow. As I got older, any "feminine" behavior was quickly ridiculed. Being girly was seen as weak and silly.

As far as I can recall, I was in primary school when I started thinking I was too fat. The female stars and role models I saw were all slim and pretty. Like lots of young people, when I reached puberty I was uncomfortable with my body. I was convinced I had to lose weight to be happy. My body changed, and so did the way others looked at me. I must have been 13 years old when the street harassment started. No one thought it was a big deal. Commenting on girls' bodies and criticizing them was just part of life. Sex education left a lot to be desired in terms of educating young people about relationships, consent and anatomy, and all my friends experienced the consequences of that.

It took me a while to realize that, as girls, we are treated differently. The things that happen might seem like isolated cases, but they all add up to a system of inequality, a system that targets people for the sole reason that they were born a girl. But with awareness, we see that we're not alone. This gives us strength and so much hope. Every day people fight for equality. We can't take anything for granted these days. We must broaden our horizons and open our minds. There are some urgent issues regarding the status of girls. And these issues concern us all. Whether you're a girl, a boy, non-binary or trans, I hope this book will open your eyes to the feminist struggle, inspire you to start a conversation and give you the courage to take your own kind of action.

Want to Learn More?

HERE ARE SOME SUGGESTIONS TO HELP YOU DIG A LITTLE DEEPER INTO THE ISSUES THIS BOOK TOUCHES ON AND FIGURE OUT THE NEXT STEPS YOU CAN TAKE. REMEMBER, THESE ARE ONLY SUGGESTIONS, SO FEEL FREE TO DO YOUR OWN RESEARCH TOO!

KANEILA IN NEPAL

ASSOCIATION—CARE stands up for women's rights in Nepal and campaigns against poverty and the period taboo.

ASSOCIATION—The Cup Foundation (thecup.org) provides reusable menstrual cups to young women and educates boys about respect and gender equality.

BOOK—*Period Power* by Nadya Okamoto, published by Simon & Schuster Books for Young Readers, is a manifesto on menstruation.

FILM—*Period. End of Sentence.* (2018) is an Oscar-winning documentary about women in India and their campaign to end menstrual precariousness and raise awareness about periods.

JADE IN FRANCE

ASSOCIATION—The National Association to Advance Fat Acceptance is a nonprofit organization dedicated to protecting the rights of fat people.

BOOK—*Fat Chance, Charlie Vega* by Crystal Maldonado, published by Holiday House, is a young adult novel about our relationships with our families, our bodies and ourselves.

BOOK—*The (Other) F Word: A Celebration of the Fat & Fierce*, edited by Angie Manifredi and published by Amulet Books, is a collection of art, poetry, essays and fashion tips about body image and fat acceptance.

FILM—*Fattitude* (2017) is a documentary co-created by Lindsey Averill and Viridiana Lieberman.

TV SERIES—*My Mad Fat Diary* (2013) is about a teenager, Rae, the complicated relationship she has with her body, and her mental health.

MAHNOOSH IN AFGHANISTAN

ACTIVIST—Sonita Alizadeh is an Afghan rapper and activist who speaks out against forced marriages.

ASSOCIATIONS—There's an urgent need to help women in Afghanistan. Afghanistan Libre, NEGAR, Women for Women International and UNICEF are all accepting donations to the cause.

BOOK—*One Half from the East* by Nadia Hashimi, published by Harper Collins, tells the story of a girl living as a bacha posh.

FILM—*The Breadwinner* (2017) is an animated film that paints an artful picture of life for a girl in Afghanistan under the Taliban regime.

MAKENA IN KENYA

ASSOCIATION—Orchid Project campaigns against all forms of FGM.

ASSOCIATION—Reteti Elephant Sanctuary is always in need of support to continue its work to save the elephants.

ASSOCIATION—The Samburu Girls Foundation advocates for Samburu girls to have access to education and campaigns against female genital mutilation (FGM) and forced marriages.

BOOK—*Secrets of the Henna Girl* by Sufiya Ahmed, published by Puffin, is a young adult novel that explores the illegal practice of forced marriages in the UK.

FILM—*Le Clitoris* (2016) is a short animated film about the clitoris by filmmaker Lori Malépart-Traversy.

LUISA IN MEXICO

ACTIVIST—Imelda Marrufo Nava works with the association Red Mesa de Mujeres. As a lawyer and an activist, she has documented and shared the names and stories of the many victims of femicide in Ciudad Juárez, Mexico.

ASSOCIATION—Amnesty International campaigns for human rights. The organization stands by the activist Wendy Galarza in her fight for justice in response to the police crackdown on feminist protests in Cancún.

ASSOCIATION—The collective Las Hijas de Violencia uses punk rock to combat street harassment. They protest in the streets by firing guns filled with confetti at men who harass them.

ASSOCIATION—Tahirih Justice Center is a nonprofit organization that helps immigrants escape gender-based violence.

PHOTOGRAPHER—Andrea Murcia is a photographer and journalist in Mexico City. Her photos document the feminist struggle with a powerful punch.

ACKNOWLEDGMENTS

Thank you very much for reading this book. I hope it resonates with you at least a little.

Thank you, Marianne. I would never have been determined enough to write this book without you.

Infinite thanks to my French publisher, Les Éditions du Ricochet, and to my super team—Natalie, Gabriella and Reutty—for their trust and support, as well as for believing in this project.

Louise, *Born a Girl* started with you, so thank you. And thanks to everyone who first followed my project when I was still in school.

Thank you to my girlfriends and my beloved little family for encouraging me and being so enthusiastic.

More than anything, special thanks to Laury Anne at CARE, Julien at Plan International, Wanjiru at the Samburu Girls Foundation, and Natali and her students at Girls Who Code for their great help.

And thank you to the many girls who responded to my survey and shared their stories with me.

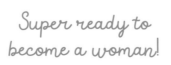

Super ready to become a woman!

INDEX

Text and illustrations © Alice Dussutour 2024
Translation copyright © David Warriner 2024

English edition published in 2024 in Canada and the United States
by Orca Book Publishers.
orcabook.com

Original edition, *Naître fille*, published in French © Les Éditions du Ricochet, 2022.

Library and Archives Canada Cataloguing in Publication
Title: Born a girl : it takes courage / by Alice Dussutour ;
translated from the French by David Warriner.
Other titles: Naître fille. English
Names: Dussutour, Alice, author. | Warriner, David (Linguist), translator.
Description: Translation of: Naître fille. | Includes index.
Identifiers: Canadiana (print) 2023044136X | Canadiana (ebook) 20230441424 |
ISBN 9781459838987 (hardcover) | ISBN 9781459838994 (PDF) | ISBN 9781459839007 (EPUB)
Subjects: LCSH: Young women—Social conditions—Juvenile literature. | LCSH: Girls—Social conditions—Juvenile literature. |
LCSH: Women—Social conditions—Juvenile literature. | LCSH: Feminism—Juvenile literature.
Classification: LCC HQ798 .D8713 2024 | DDC j305.235/2—dc23

Library of Congress Control Number: 2023937664

Summary: This illustrated book for young readers shares the stories of
five girls growing up around the world and some of the injustices they face.

Orca Book Publishers is committed to reducing the consumption of nonrenewable resources in the
production of our books. We make every effort to use materials that support a sustainable future.

Orca Book Publishers gratefully acknowledges the support for its publishing programs provided by
the following agencies: the Government of Canada, the Canada Council for the Arts and the
Province of British Columbia through the BC Arts Council and the Book Publishing Tax Credit.

The author and publisher have made every effort to ensure that the information in this book was correct
at the time of publication. The author and publisher do not assume any liability for any loss, damage,
or disruption caused by errors or omissions. Every effort has been made to trace copyright holders and to obtain
their permission for the use of copyrighted material. The publisher apologizes for any errors or omissions and would
be grateful if notified of any corrections that should be incorporated in future reprints or editions of this book.

Cover and interior artwork by Alice Dussutour
Translated by David Warriner

Printed and bound in South Korea.

27   26   25   24   •   1   2   3   4